Advertising
Art

Advertising Art

Time and Money-saving
Tricks of the Trade

Tony Hinwood

David & Charles : Newton Abbot

0 7153 5694 1

NC
997
H48

1/83 11. 25

89178

Set in 11/13 IBM Press Roman
and printed in Great Britain
by Redwood Press Limited Trowbridge Wiltshire
for David & Charles (Holdings) Limited
South Devon House Newton Abbot Devon

Contents

Illustrations

Illustrations

Illustrations

Illustrations

10

Foreword

One of the unique facts of the advertising art business is the difficulty in obtaining information which faces the art student. Even now, art schools consistently fail to supply their students with the sort of knowhow that modern industry demands.

Studios, agencies, creative groups and company advertising departments are usually far too busy to invest time in training inexperienced artists, and none but the potentially brilliant will get the employment they seek. The keen student soon becomes disenchanted with his chosen profession, and may be forced to turn elsewhere for work.

Even those already employed in art studios find it difficult to learn the tricks and professional 'wrinkles' of the trade, and the reluctance of the top professionals to reveal techniques that have taken years to acquire is understandable. In the competitive pressures and traditional insecurity of today's business world, it is these tricks that are the most closely guarded.

The author feels that this concept is both short-sighted and naive, relegating the creative artist to the role of a craftsman with little chance of reaching the higher income brackets of the management league.

This book aims to help the artist speed up his mastery of the craft in order to aid his climb up the ladder. For the ambitious, it could be a shot-in-the-arm, and for the man who prefers to stay 'on the board' it will make life a little easier. The contents are aimed at the artist who is already art-school trained and familiar with the tools of the trade but lacks the tricks.

1: Equipment

FILLING A RULING PEN

Use the dropper attached to the cap, and apply about ¼in of ink between the pen blades. Clean off the surplus ink with blotting paper or an absorbent rag.

If you are using poster paint, apply it with a brush but make sure that it is the right consistency for an even flow. Trial and error will soon determine the right blend of colour and water — make it the consistency of cream.

CURING A STUBBORN RULING PEN

The ruling pen can create problems if it is not looked after properly. Clean it out regularly with a piece of blotting paper; this prevents the medium from drying or thickening up in the pen (the main reason for poor ink flow). If pen blades lose their sharpness, they should be carefully honed on a carborundum stone.

THE DOUBLE RULE PEN

A useful tool for drawing parallel ink lines is the double-ruling pen — two ruling pens joined together by a common handle; it allows two lines to be drawn simultaneously and with varying thicknesses of line.

PREVENTING A VALVE-TYPE PEN FROM DRYING OUT

Put a swab of water-moistened cottonwool into the cap, then replace the cap carefully to keep out the air. This will keep the needle free, but make sure you check from time to time that the swab is kept damp. Alternatively you could make a tightly fitting cap from durable polythene. Merely place the two edges between metal rulers (like a sandwich) and then run a flame along the edges to create a seam by burning the film. A piece of damp cottonwool in the end of the polythene cap will ensure a free-working needle valve to your pens.

PRECAUTIONS WITH PAINT

When you buy paint in jars you will find that the manufacturers have used a liquid on top of the paint, to keep it moist. This is usually glycerine. Always remove this before using; if you do not, the paint will not dry properly and will leave a sticky surface.

PREVENTING PAINT FROM GOING HARD

To prevent paint from drying up in the jar when it has to stand for long periods, simply turn it upside down. The air pressure creates an airtight seal that keeps the paint moist.

SOFTENING PAINT IN THE TUBE

If you have the old problem of paint going hard in the tube, just place the tube in boiling water for about a minute, and you will find it usable again.

KEEPING THE PAINT FLOWING

When paint crawls, and refuses to cover the area due to grease or the nature of the materials, try using a little soap or liquid detergent in your paint container. Alternatively, a quick rub over the area with a kneaded eraser may suffice.

WORKING OVER WET PAINT

Although not used as often as in former years, a handrest can be a valuable time-saver. It consists of a strip of thin wood (satin walnut is ideal) about 15in to 18in long by 4in broad, supported on two battens, one at each end of the rest, which raise the strip ¼in off the working surface.

As a further refinement, and to avoid possible scratching of your working surface, add a piece of felt or baize cloth to the batten strips; or small rubber beads will do this and also restrict movement so that accidents are cut to a minimum.

With practice the feel of the rest will become second nature, permitting a greater measure of freedom to work over wet areas — a useful point where the familiar rush jobs are concerned.

Another advantage is that the edge can be used as a ruler, particularly when filling in flat body-colour areas.

CONSISTENCY TRIALS

Art mediums like poster paint, ink or acrylic colours require regular testing of the load for consistency and control. Instead of reducing the edge of your board to a mass of dirty brush strokes, try laying newspapers down over the drawing board before you start. They sop up the excess paint far more quickly, and reduce the risk of 'elbow transfer'.

DRYING WORK QUICKLY

The simplest way to speed up the process of drying is to fan the artwork with a piece of card, or use an old portable electric fan or a hair-dryer. Electric lamps and heaters can accelerate drying time, but can also result in cockling. Good old-fashioned blotting paper is extremely useful for drying off ink, paint and similar wet agents. Wrap it around a card tube to make a simple roller, and fix it with cellulose tape. This method is more efficient than using it in sheet form.

A BETTER WHITE FOR FINISHED ART

In a damp atmosphere or when water is accidentally spilled onto finished art, the white often becomes soft and vulnerable to smudging. Apart from spraying the job with a fixative, you may find that Casein waterproof colours work well, dry fairly quickly and are unaffected by dampness. Casein colours are obtainable from any good art supplier. Do not, however, use this colour in a spray gun as it dries too quickly and will clog up the nozzle.

NEUTRAL WASHES

To make a neutral wash in monochrome work, mix various proportions of blue and brown ink, altering the percentages to achieve the tone required.

KEEPING BRUSHES CLEAN

A few small drops of detergent in the water pot will clean brushes quicker when you rinse them. The pot will remain cleaner, avoid accumulated scum, and the colours will run better, especially when painting on a greasy surface.

KEEPING BRUSHES IN GOOD CONDITION

Take a strip of gummed paper, wet each brush with water and roll and twirl it into the gum so that the gummy solution is absorbed by the hairs; with the finger and thumb then shape it into a point. When it dries out, the point is retained and the brush will keep its shape. To use again, simply wash the brush in clean water to remove the gum.

FIXATIVES

Originally designed as a medium for fixing charcoal and pastel layouts, the standard colourless fixative has been assigned to many new tasks since the decline in popularity of pastel. The current popularity of felt-tip pen markers has been a major factor in this, but the markers themselves can also benefit from a limited use of fixatives. For example: overall spray produces a slight softening of body colours, and will give a slight gloss to an otherwise matt surface. Do not overdo it, or the colours will become streaky.

REMOVING FIXATIVE

If you forget to remove pencil lines before spraying with a fixative, make a cotton-wool swab and apply it to a paint brush. Pour some fixative on to the swab, and with smooth, regular strokes, carefully rub the surface to dissolve the spray. You should be able to remove enough fixative to allow you to rub out the offending pencil lines before spraying the job over again.

USING A CARBORUNDUM STONE

Keep a carborundum stone to hand and you will never have to worry about how to sharpen the edges of your instruments.

When you buy a new stone, be sure to temper it by saturating it in molten petroleum jelly. You won't need to use any oil on it after this treatment as the jelly will act as a lubricant and prevent pieces of metal from becoming engrained in the stone.

KEEPING A POINT ON YOUR PENCILS

An engineer's file (or a nail file) is a handy tool to have around for sharpening your layout pencils into a chisel edge. It saves buying sandpaper-blocks and could last indefinitely. Keep it clean with a wire brush and by tapping to remove the graphite dust. If the grooves fill up with graphite, use boiling water and soap to restore them to their original condition.

MAKING A SCRIBER

Take your clutch pencil (the sort that holds pencil leads) and insert a discarded compass needle. If it slips through the grippers, take a small length of plastic flex, pull out the strands of wire and use this as a sleeve around the needle.

MASKING WITH THE DOUBLE-L METHOD

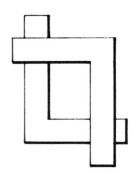

Cut two large L-shapes from card, about 12in by 12in. When placed together they form a square or rectangle which can be moved around to find the best area for cropping a photograph or illustration. When you have adjusted the horizontal and vertical areas to your liking, tape them in position to indicate the exact proportions you require at the plating stage.

PERSPECTIVE AIDS

It is now possible to buy sheets with radiating perspective lines already printed on them. However, if you are stuck, cut an arc in a piece of card, large enough to take the butt-end of a T-square. Slide the T-square along the card arc, so that the perspective lines are automatically drawn and completely accurate.

UTILISING PRINT OFFCUTS

If you cut out the centre portion of a photo for paste-up, hold on to the offcut. This gives you an exact-size template for pasting-up, and cuts unnecessary cleaning to a minimum.

CUTTING CIRCLES IN PAPER AND CARD

The simplest way to cut neat circles is to buy one of the instruments specially designed for the job. If they prove hard to obtain, an equally effective device can be made by adapting a springbow compass. Simply break or saw off one of the nibs of the pen part, then sharpen up the remaining one into a cutting blade on a carborundum stone. The smaller-size compass is ideal for paper and thin card, but if you want to cut cartonboard or strawboard it will pay to adapt a larger one.

USING A REDUCING GLASS

If you don't have access to a camera tracing machine you may find it difficult to visualise what your artwork will look like on reduction. A reducing glass may solve this problem for you. First determine the ratio of reduction, for example: 2:1. Draw two marks, 2in apart, on the artwork; then make two additional marks, 1in apart, on your reducing glass (a Chinagraph pencil works well). By moving the glass away from the artwork until the marks correspond, you will see exactly what the reduction will look like.

POLYESTER FILM

This is ideal for overlays; it is stable, accepts fixative without distortion, can be used many times over and permits remarkably clear pencil lines. Instant lettering looks better and applies well on the matt surface. Ruby photo opaque tape is also easy to use on double-matt film as it does not curl.

SELF-ADHESIVE COLOURED PLASTIC FILM

This can be used where a large area of colour is wanted for many purposes, especially display work. Dry-transfer lettering is easy to apply and fixative takes well. This film is sold in many hardware stores for domestic use.

SHARPENING SCISSORS

An effective way of sharpening scissor edges is to use the neck of a glass bottle as a strop. Use a cutting action a few times on the neck; fairly firm pressure is needed and practice will tell you whether you are using the right amount.

SAVING MONEY ON PAPER

Whilst it is standard professional practice to use the best materials money can buy, there are many occasions when substantial savings can be made, especially when artwork goes direct to production and avoids the necessity of showing a beautifully flapped piece of art to the client.

Black and white illustrations, for example, can be drawn as well on layout tissue as on expensive Bristol board. The art can be photographed later for bromide prints if necessary, but to prevent cockling it, will require mounting if you intend to fill in large areas of body colour.

Heavier line work can be done on chalk-coated pulp boards which are very smooth and accept line and ink readily. They cost a fraction of the price of standard illustration board, and have an added advantage in that corrections can be made by scratching away the chalk surface. Great savings can be made with this board on a multi-page assignment such as a book or brochure. The board can be ordered ready-cut to the trim-size of book pages, which permits you to make it up in a ring-binder format. Choose an appropriate-size binder, punch holes to match, and you will have saved more than half the cost of conventional board.

When grouping line prints for a multiple exposure shot, why mount them on expensive board when a cheap strawboard will do? The resulting bromide print will not show the texture or quality of the mount, and you have saved on the expense without affecting the quality of the print.

SIMPLIFYING THE REPEAT JOB

For regular monthly assignments like house magazines, newsletters, statistical reports etc, where the basic format is changed only slightly for each new edition, use the standard format idea.

This consists of a normal illustration board with the trim marks, folding and creasing lines and register marks ruled in ink, together with any permanent features such as the masthead, page numbers, column heads or company logo etc. The type-grid is marked out in blue pencil with any specifications included, and the entire board is then covered with transparent acetate so that the column lines and margins are clearly visible.

The format is then ready to pass from artist to printer to client and back, in a continuously flowing production sequence, with the overlay acting as a mount for the regular monthly copy changes.

BLUE-PENCIL TRANSFER SHEETS

A blue pencil, if rubbed on to the back of a sheet of detail paper, will make a useful medium for tracing work. The blue will not reproduce and it saves cleaning-up time in an emergency. A soft lead pencil or graphite stick can also be used, but it can be messy. A better method is to use powdered graphite (obtainable at most hardware stores); pour a quantity on the back of your trace so that it spreads easily. Shake the powder to cover the area evenly, then blow away the surplus to leave a fine deposit of graphite dust. Now take a piece of cottonwool and spread the graphite smoothly over the surface, working from the centre outwards in all directions. When complete, there should be no surplus dust, and you will have a tracing sheet capable of transferring ultra-fine, soft grey lines that show up well and are easy to erase. You can, of course, buy ready-made transfer sheets from art shops, but similar sheets can also be created by rubbing conte crayon on tissue paper and washing the surface with methylated spirit on a cottonwool pad. This makes the tissue paper absorb the crayon.

EMERGENCY 'FRISKET' PAPER

In an emergency, dry mounting tissue is ideal for photo-retouching masks. You can apply this in the usual way with rubber cement.

CLEANING ACETATE FILM

To remove errors and generally clean off blemishes efficiently, use a sharpened matchstick or wooden toothpick. These make-do tools are better than a metal blade as they avoid scratching the surface. If you have to remove solid areas of black ink, try a cottonwool swab dipped in warm soapy water, rub hard and keep changing the swabs.

CLEANING POLYESTER FILM

This is best carried out with a dilute solution of ammonia, but it can be used straight from the bottle. Make a swab from cottonwool on the end of a paint brush, and use sweeping strokes to remove errors, etc. Dry it off with blotting paper if you are in a hurry.

CLEANING ARTWORK

To clean off surplus rubber solution, deposit some of the gum on a dish and allow it to dry, then roll it into a hard tight ball so that it acts as a rubber and picks up the excess gum around the edges of your work. Or wrap adhesive tape around your finger, tacky side out, and wipe quickly and lightly across the area to be cleaned. Renew tape as it becomes dirty. It will remove rubber cement, pencil marks, mechanical tints or transfer lettering.

CLEANING DRAWING INSTRUMENTS

Try ordinary toothpaste for this chore; it is a poor abrasive and will not scratch your perspex squares, rulers or templates.

A COVER FOR YOUR DRAWING BOARD

Avoid leaving artwork exposed for lengthy periods of time, as paste-up mechanicals attract dust and dirt like a magnet. A large sheet of black polythene pinned or taped to the top edge of the board will help to prevent fading by sunlight and keep the artwork dust-free. If you forget to cover your board remove dust particles with a soft duster. Brushes, other than anti-static brushes, can cause static electricity which attracts rather than repels the dust.

CHECKING ALIGNMENT WITHOUT A DRAWING BOARD

The grid-line guide that printers use for checking paste-up accuracy is a very expensive piece of equipment. An efficient and inexpensive facsimile can be made by photographing standard graph paper, and then producing a positive transparency of the image, thus making a useful tool of the trade.

The main advantage of this tool is its portability, which enables you to check artwork while out of the studio — it weighs nothing, and depending on the size you make it, will fit in most normal-size artcases.

KEEPING ART BOARD RIGID

For better rigidity of the art board, use drawing-board pins for securing the work. If you use tape, the board may lift and, with constant usage, could be out of true to your original datum lines. For quick jobs and layouts, take drafting tape and position it diagonally across the top corners.

PROTECTING ARTWORK

Artwork can easily be damaged in the post or by careless messenger boys. Once it leaves the artist's hands, there is little he can do to protect it other than to pack it flat, with stiff card on both sides to prevent bending. Never send artwork rolled up if it can be avoided, but if it must be rolled, roll it on the outside of the tube and then protect the surface of the roll with more packing. Finger marks, smudges on type proofs, tears and other disasters can all be avoided by flapping the artwork with tissue, and then a heavier protective cover paper. Avoid marking the back of photographs in pencil or ball-point pen, as the impression may come through on the picture side and reproduce in the printing. Use a felt-tip pen or soft crayon instead.

CHECKING EQUIPMENT

Before using setsquares or T-squares on work requiring accuracy, the experienced artist checks the following points:
1. Is the square true? Old age and continuous handling may have rendered it useless. Even a new square is not necessarily perfect so make a spot check before using it.
2. Burred corners caused by accidentally dropping the square are another common problem, preventing the tool from lying flush against the T-square. Shave away the burr with a razor blade or scalpel and it will be as good as new.
3. Expansion and contraction need careful watching, especially under high temperatures. To check, lay the square over a sheet of paper against your T-square in the normal way and draw a vertical line with a pencil the full length of the setsquare without moving the T-square. Turn the setsquare over, so that the side you drew against is facing the line, and draw another line. If it does not come parallel with the original line, the square is out of true and should be rapidly consigned to the waste basket.

SPECIAL EQUIPMENT

There are times when it pays to buy ultra-specialised equipment. For example, the compass that has a cutter device capable of producing perfect discs will pay for itself for the artist who specialises in point-of-sale design.

BOOK REFERENCES

Keeping a good reference library is mandatory for all creative studios and freelance designers; magazine references can be cut out and filed, but you naturally want to avoid mutilating books. The simple answer is to keep a card-index system, indicating subject, medium, book title, chapter or section and page number. Keep a card for each book, or divide the complete library into cross-references.

2: *Layout and basic shapes*

BASIC RULES FOR LAYOUT

All rules were made to be broken and the experienced layout man will know when to forget the book. However, certain basic principles fit the bread-and-butter type ad even when the copy and art elements are supplied.

Copywriters may suggest a layout verbally or by means of a simple scratch-pad doodle, but do not allow them to dictate one; the art department will frequently have a better idea. Layout and copy elements must be visualised as a single design entity and not merely as a design plus a block of copy! Layouts, whether based on a copywriter's suggestion or originated entirely by the art department, should concentrate on: drama; balance; good taste; simplicity – plus generous use of white space.

Colour layouts should be presented whenever possible and account executives encouraged to sell them in preference to black-and-white.

Photographs carry conviction and lend all advertisements something of a 'case history' quality. They are not always suitable for newspapers owing to reproduction problems on low-quality newsprint, but their use should always be considered for magazine ads on good-quality stock.

All the above principles apply equally to direct-mail shots, except that the body copy may be a little longer if necessary.

SKETCHING OUT VISUALS

When preparing a rough working visual, work the design out in pencil, then tear it off and slip it under the top sheet of your layout pad. You can safely use your marker on the top sheet, leaving the guide sheet to protect the other sheets on your pad.

FELT-TIP MARKER TRICKS

With current layout trends moving away from the tight, almost printed look, the greatest single advantage of felt-tip markers is the time they save in rendering layouts. Other mediums like pastel, poster paint and water-colours require time-consuming care to keep the work looking fresh and clean. The following techniques will be useful to all artists who use felt-tip markers for visualising.

The standard (four-way-tip) marker makes it possible to achieve a wide variety of strokes ranging from hairline to bold, merely by turning the marker on edge and drawing with sharp corners, or with the full width of the felt.

To cover solid areas, two or three methods can be used, depending on the

26

effect required. Straight-ruled, broad, slightly overlapping lines result in a slick, regimented style. Rubbing the marker back and forth in scribble fashion so that the ink floods and merges produces a smooth, slightly blotchy tone free of hard edges. This technique is particularly useful in rendering full-colour work, as the

blending of different coloured markers while still wet produces beautiful tonal effects similar to four-colour halftones.

A dry-brush effect is achieved by making quick, light strokes on textured paper. The possibilities are limitless.

When making layouts on the pad, sketch out your concept on the top sheet then slip it under a fresh sheet to act as a guide for the finished rough. The preliminary sketch will also act as a barrier to prevent the marker ink from bleeding through and spoiling the sheets underneath.

Where both sides of a sheet have to be rendered, as in leaflets, folders and booklets, select a paper that is easy to control and thick enough to contain the ink without allowing bleed-through. If you still have problems, do your layout on two sheets of cartridge and paste them together. If you paste layout tissue directly on to a cartridge-paper backing, be very careful to keep the rubber-solution clean, as marks will show through the layout paper.

THE SOFT-FOCUS LOOK TO FELT-TIP WORK

Should you wish to remove a hard edge from your layout the following technique is effective and produces a soft-focus look. Select a pale-grey marker of the wide-nib kind and quickly go over the working area to dampen it. Immediately work the other colours into the same area, blending them carefully to achieve a pleasing effect. Experiment first on a spare piece of similar stock to get the feel of the technique and avoid spoiling the job. The same method will work equally well with the layout of graduated greys.

Remember, there are two kinds of felt-tip markers — the spirit-ink sort, and the watercolour drawing sticks. With the former, there is a tendency for the inks to bleed through thin paper, but with water-colour markers, this problem does not arise, unless they are diluted with water; choose the right type of marker for each job and you will have no trouble.

Note: Whilst blending is a fairly simple matter with spirit inks, it is not so easy with water colour markers unless you add some water, and wash the colours together with a brush.

AVOIDING INK TRANSFER FROM FELT-TIPS

One of the problems of felt-tip markers is the ease with which they mess up triangles, T-Squares and rulers. A simple way to cure this is by taping the edge of your instruments with a strip of masking tape. It saves you having to clean off the edges each time they are used, and after use it is an easy matter to strip off the old tape and replace it with new. Another problem solved by this trick is the transfer of a dark ink into a light felt nib. This happens when the light colour is used while the edge is still wet from a dark colour. Change the tape after each colour and you will have no worries.

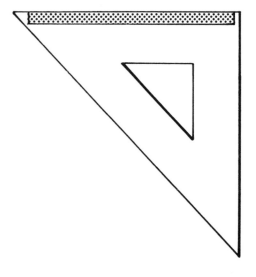

RENDERING HALFTONES WITH A FELT PEN

Photography and illustration rendering can be made easier by indicating the broad flat area first. Use the broad side of your felt pen and flood a light colour into the main masses of your picture to give you an idea of how the elements will drop in; next build up the medium tones to strengthen the contrast values and choose different colours for the subject matter, eg blue for sky, green for grass and trees, 'flesh'

28

and grey for figures or townscapes. If mistakes are made at this stage, they can be quickly arrested before you drop in the bolder, darker colours and sketch in the details. (These should be done with a Pentel or any fine-writing fibre-tip pen.) Remember to lay in the flat 'body colours' first — it is far quicker this way than trying to sketch the line detail straight off without any guide.

LETTERING THE LAYOUT

The ability to render crisp professional lettering can be a visualiser's prime asset, and a skilful interpretation of the art director's rough can reap big dividends in the career of the budding art director.

One of the basic points of layout lettering is to get the feel of the typefaces quickly, then indicate its main characteristics. Show how and where the bold or light parts of the type occur. For example, the relationship between the thicks and thins must be kept constant. Keeping an even colour is equally important — which means that no character should appear darker or lighter than another, and your ascenders and descenders should be both vertical and parallel.

In a nutshell, if the lettering is carefully rendered, it should match the typeface. A shortcut to rapid type rendering is the T-square method. Parallel guidelines can be eliminated, resulting in a straight, neat-looking line of type which can be taken to any degree of finish. To operate the T-square method, draw your vertical strokes straight down to hit the top of the T-square edge; the fact that some characters are normally flat is useful, but if the Os and Cs etc tend to look flattened, corrections can be made later on.

Rough out the line quickly on tracing paper, then use it as an underlay guide for spacing and size. At this stage, keep checking each character as you go to ensure that the body height remains constant. The base of each character is controlled by your T-square. When the line is complete, go back to round off any square-looking letters and add the descenders. With plenty of practice it will become routine; remember to choose the right lettering tool for each job.

Always have the relevant alphabet to hand until you become experienced enough to visualise the type without using reference material.

SCALING A LAYOUT TO FIT DIFFERENT SIZES

If you are asked to prepare a layout to fit various different type-areas, always draw

29

in the areas first on detail paper. You can then scale to a common area (usually half-up), and order your repros or prints to fit this common scale. Flaps will probably be necessary for any odd sizes over the common area, or a paper mask for the non-scale areas.

KEEPING LAYOUTS CLEAN

Accidents are inevitable, and pencil smudges, thumbprints, and other marks endemic to the business are often hard to remove. A liberal application of rubber-solution could be the answer to this problem. Brush a small amount across the offending mark and leave until it is tacky. Next, rub over the area with a ball of dry rubber-solution until all the surface solution is removed. The marks will adhere to the rubber and disappear as the gum is removed. A final clean-off can be done with a normal eraser.

PRESENTATION LAYOUTS AT SPEED

When creative work requires a highly professional, printed look, the following tricks may prove useful: make a pencil layout of the ad as a positional guide to show how the elements fit in, then mount them up as indicated. Headlines can be lettered in with dry-transfer lettering. The body copy may be ruled lines, typeset or rendered with 'Greeking' (body type on self-adhesive sheets). Line illustrations sketched in felt pen, and photographs taken with a polaroid, complete the package. If a company logo is required, use a cutting from an old pull, paste-up the complete assembly and, when finished, order photoprints from your photographic supplier, giving him specific instructions to paint out unwanted lines at the negative stage. The result is a glossy, expensive-looking print which closely approximates to the printed piece. If the ads are for a client conference, order duplicate copies for mounting in folders together with the copy recommendations.

If the layout is in colour, adjust it at the paste-up stage to allow for the addition of body colour and reversed-out elements. For example, where you would indicate a solid area as black on a one-colour job, leave it blank so that you can drop in the colour when the prints return from the photographer.

CORRECTING LAYOUTS

To make the sort of layout correction that will not show up at the client presentation, tape a sheet of detail paper over the affected part and draw in the amendments so that they match in with the rest of the layout. Cut through the detail into the original and insert a knife to lift the top sheet so that the incorrect part can be removed. Once it is removed, merely replace the corrected part so that it drops neatly in to place. Finish off the job by taping the reverse side to hold the amendment in position.

REPEAT PAGE LAYOUT

When you have a large number of standard layout sheets to work on with headings, sub-headings and ruled lines, for example, place three or four pages together on your drawing board so that they are accurately lined up. Put all relevant markings on the board by the side of your work in order to repeat all the guide lines and save measuring time.

ENLARGING OR REDUCING IN PROPORTION

A drawing can be enlarged without the aid of a projector just as efficiently (though not as quickly) by the following methods.

Method 1 Use the diagonal-line principle to find the desired proportions, then divide the rectangle into squares or geometric patterns, as in the diagram overleaf. (The bigger the squares the bigger the final enlargement.) Use tracing paper or film, then fasten the lined sheet over your otiginal with bulldog clips so that it stays put. Repeat the squares or diagonals on your original and follow the details according to the locating points. A good trick is to number each line on the art and on the grid-trace, so that they correspond with each other.

Method 2 This method may appear complicated, in fact the technique is quite simple. Lay tracing paper over the work, and draw an oblong or square around the extremities. Draw a diagonal across the page and draw the enlarged or reduced area on the same sheet so that it is in proportion by the diagonal. Next draw an outline of the object, and note its main features such as shoulder levels, elbow positions, etc, and project horizontal lines to the boundary of the original square or rectangle.

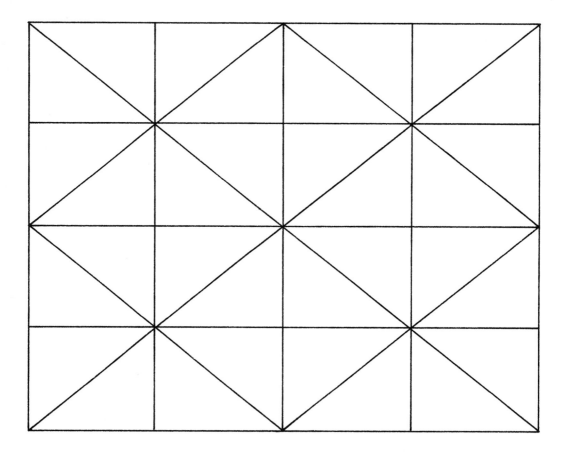

Assuming that you are enlarging the drawing for purposes of the description, line-up the ruler to the boundary original on a locating line from the corner where you have taken the diagonal on the original. Project the enlarging line to the boundary of the enlarged area, and mark a point. From this point draw a horizontal in another colour, say a red ball-point pen. Repeat this process, both horizontally and vertically, until you have built-up a new grid enlarged from the original. Simply connect the points according to the grid and a super-accurate scale drawing will result.

PLOTTING CHARTS THE EASY WAY

A good idea to simplify chart work is to use a plotting card. A typical example would be a 3in x 5in card with two lines ruled across it equal to the space between the horizontal grid lines of the chart. This space can then be further subdivided to represent smaller units. The scale makes it much easier to plot how far each of the figures comes above its respective grid lines.

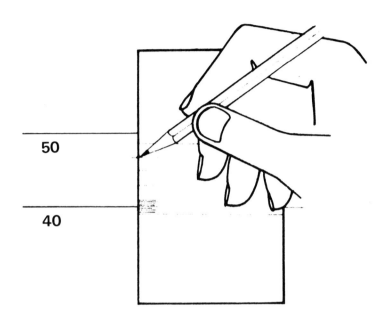

50

40

PIE-CHARTS

The 'pie' or round chart calls for a diagram based on the cutting of a pie into slices, symbolising percentages. As a complete circle contains 360°, it will therefore represent 100 per cent. If it is divided into half, each circle contains 180° or a representation of 50 per cent. If each half is again divided in half, each quarter will contain 90° or 25 per cent. One per cent will therefore equal 3.6° and simple calculations are all that is

33

necessary to construct the chart.

Here is an example for clarity: say that the percentages are 25-40-35 (the total must always be 100); merely multiply each figure by 3.6 to find the number of degrees to determine the positions on a protractor. The final percentage figure in the series will, of course, position itself automatically, thus 25 x 3.6 = 90, 40 x 3.6 = 144 and 35 x 3.6 = 126. The answers are the number of degrees (and by adding them together we get 360°).

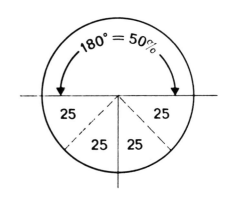

DRAWING AN ELLIPSE

Ellipse templates are useless beyond a certain size, so if you need a really large oval, use the following geometric method. Let us suppose you need an oval 5 x 3in. On your tracing pad draw an infinite line A-C, and across it at right angles, a vertical line B-D, giving point O. Set your compass at 2½in, ie half the desired width of the oval and at centre O describe a circle. Repeat this with your compass set at 1½in, ie half the required depth of your oval. Next divide a quarter of the outer circle into any number of segments, as at a, draw lines

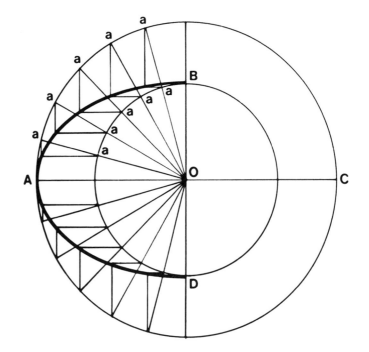

parallel to A-C and then to B-D.
Where these parallels intersect, draw
the curve of your oval. Only a
quarter of the oval needs working
on, as the remaining quarters can
be traced off.
This next method is even quicker.
On your pad draw lines A-C and
B-D giving point O, as before. Then
take a strip of paper or thin card, as
E, and mark lines 1 and 2, 1½in
apart, and lines 1 and 3, 2½in apart.
Place this card on lines A-C and B-D
so that line 2 is touching line A-C
and line 3 is touching B-D. Mark on
the tracing a point opposite line 1.
By shifting the strip, and always
keeping line 2 touching A-C, with
line 3 touching B-D, any number of
points can be marked opposite 1, as
shown in the diagram. If you make
a template from card following
the tracing, you may then repeat
the ovals as often as you wish.

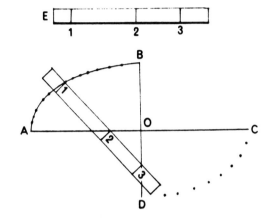

An even simpler method is as follows. Cut a piece of paper fractionally larger
than the intended size of your oval. Fold it in half, and then in half again, so that
the paper will be one quarter the original size. Make sure that the edges of the
paper are parallel and do not overlap. (The two folded edges should form a right
angle.) Next, measure from the folded corner of the paper, half the height of the
oval required, and from the same corner half the width, and tick off. Between
these two points describe an arc which will represent a quarter of the oval. This
line can be impressed through to the other folds of the paper underneath so as to
complete the ellipse. Open out the paper, and make corrections where necessary to
the key line or cut through the four sections to separate them. Either way, care
must be taken when drawing the first curve, or the final result will look more like
a diamond than an oval. The folds in the paper correspond to the height and
breadth of the oval, so watch carefully to ensure that the curve, if continued,
would keep within the limits of these folds and not run off the sheet.

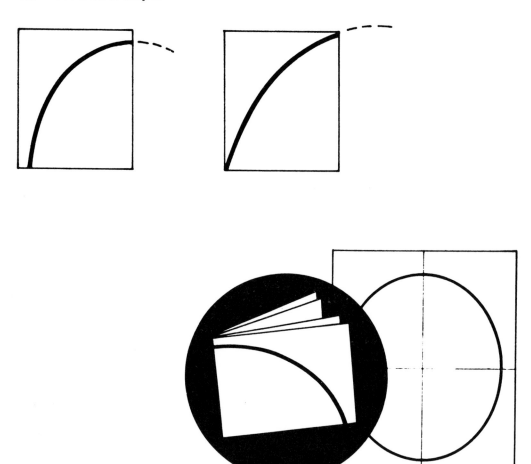

ODD-SIZE ELLIPSES WITH A TEMPLATE

When you draw a neat single-line ellipse with a template you can usually be satisfied. But if you want to thicken up the lines your problem will be how to keep the ellipse consistently thick all the way around. A simple answer to this is to obtain a small knurled-nut from your ruling pen or springbow. Just place it in the ellipse of your template and draw the line through the screw-hole with either pen-

36

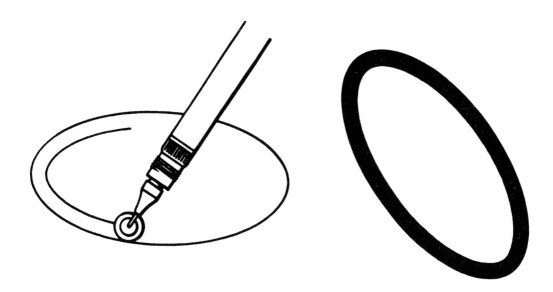

cil or needle-valve pen. Remove the screw and draw the normal ellipse — you now have a thickened guide which is simple to fill-in. To vary the thickness use different-size screws. Odd-size ellipses can also be drawn this way, and will be that much smaller than the original template ellipse. A knurled-knob screw is better than a plain metal spacer, as the ridges help to bite on the edge of the ellipse which prevents skidding.

THE EGG SHAPE

This method of forming an egg shape will prove very useful to the artman over the years. First, set out a vertical line A-B, divide it in half, at point C, and through C project a horizontal line D-E of indefinite length at right angles to A-B. From point C, where A-B and D-E intersect each other with the radius C-A or C-B, describe the circle A-B. Next, taking A and B as centres, with A-B and B-A as radii, describe the arcs B-H, A-K, and from points A and B draw through G — one of the points in which the circle A-F-B-G cuts the straight line D-E — the straight lines, A-L, B-M, respectively, cutting the arc B-H in the point O, and the arc A-K in the point N. Lastly, from G as centre, with the radius G-N or G-O, describe the arc or-quarter circle N-O which completes the exercise.

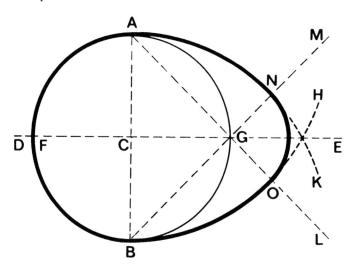

THE HEART SHAPE

The heart shape is formed by dividing line A-B into four equal parts in the points D, C, E; then from D and E as centrepoints, with radii D-A and D-B, the semicircles A-F-C, C-G-B are described, and from the same points as those centres, with radii D-B, E-A, the arcs B-L-H, A-K-H, are described. These intersect each other in H to complete the figure.

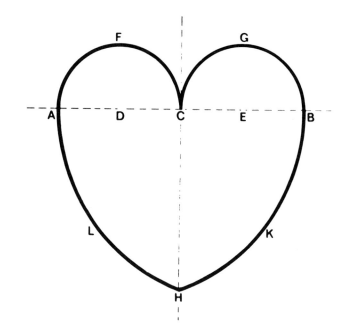

THE HOT-DOG SHAPE

Start with a straight line, A-B, equal to the outer dimensions of your intended shape. This is now divided into any number of equal parts, according to your width limit. If you want a narrow shape, a greater number of parts will be required, if wide, fewer. In this case it is divided into four equal parts in the points C, D and E as shown in the illustration. From the centre D, at the distance D-A, describe the semicircle A-H-B, and from the same centre at the distance D-C describe the semicircle C-K-E. Bisect the lines A-C, E-B, in the points F and G, and from these points as centres, with the radii F-A and G-B, describe the semicircles A-L-C, B-M-E, which complete the ends of the 'dog'.

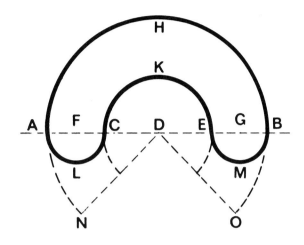

THE TUBULAR SHAPE

The difficulty of keeping a consistent thickness on tubular forms is dispelled by using this simple four-step formula:

    1. Draw a centreline guide that follows your intended shape, making sure that the construction lines are kept light.

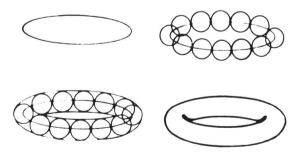

2 Draw in circles using a template or a compass — the centreline supplies the base for your compass point.

3 Draw lines that are tangent to the circles as shown.

4 Complete by cleaning away the construction lines and inking in the outline.

DRAWING A COMPASS SPIRAL

Like most geometric devices the spiral appears baffling at first sight, but becomes comparatively easy when you know how it is done; the lines must be accurately spaced or the effect will appear clumsy and uneven. The method is quite simple, providing the compass is controlled with a steady hand.

First draw a horizontal axis as shown in sketch i. Determine the two centrepoints A and B — the distance between these two points should be half the width of your intended spiral turns, as shown in the sketch. Describe a half circle, radius B-C, using B as centrepoint. Moving to centrepoint A, describe another half circle with a radius that joins D where the first circle left off, then return back to centrepoint B, and describe another half circle again from point E, and so on ad infinitum, merely altering your centrepoints. Keep going until you have enough half circles to complete the size of spiral you want.

To simplify the drawing of the circles, especially when using a springbow (ink compass), make a turntable, and swing the artwork halfway round each time you change the centrepoints. This way the half circles are drawn overhand which helps to ensure that the radii match up.

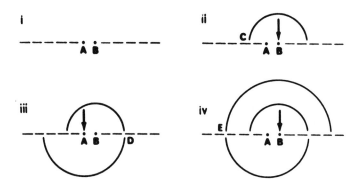

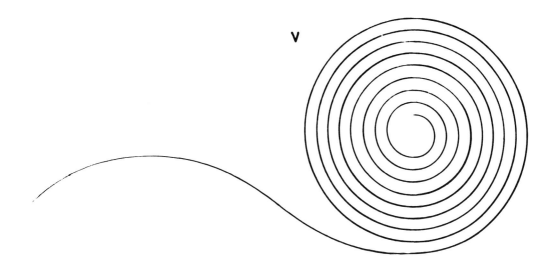

SPIRAL SHORTCUT

Draw a horizontal line in pencil then take your springbow compass and paint a white mark at a selected point on the thumbscrew. This will indicate a regular distance between the part circles that will be drawn by turning the screw.

Next, set the compass to the smallest curve of the spiral and draw a semicircle on the pencil guideline. Open the compass one or two complete turns of the screw and locate the nib on one of the ends of the semicircle, keeping the needle of the compass on the baseline. Now draw the larger semicircle in an opposite direction so that the line finishes on the baseline again. Repeat this until a spiral is drawn.

DRAWING SUPER-LARGE CIRCLES

If you do not have access to a beam compass, just push a pin into the centre of the work and make a loop at the end of a piece of string to go round the pin. At the other end of the string make another loop to take a pencil or pen. To give the correct dimension of the circle, merely shorten the string with knots.

FINDING THE CENTRE OF A PART-CIRCLE

Draw a random line A that crosses the given part of the circle. Next from its exact centre draw line B 90° to it. Now repeat this at another part of the circle, making lines C and D. Key lines B and D will cross each other at the exact centrepoint of the curve.

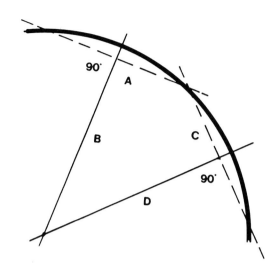

THE EQUILATERAL TRIANGLE

A six-inch equilateral triangle become a simple geometry trick with this method. Draw a six-inch line then place a 60° triangle at each end as illustrated. Project your lines upward and where they cross they will form a perfect equilateral triangle. Each side will be exactly six inches.

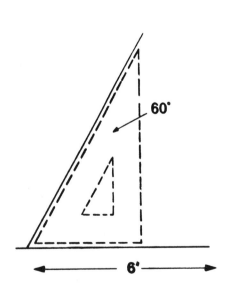

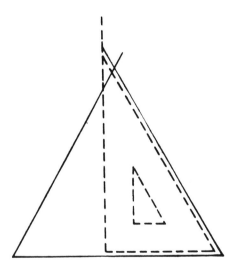

By raising your T-square up or down, virtually any size triangle can be made. The two sides will automatically equate in length with the bottom. A six-pointed star consists of two equilaterals, one inverted.

THE HEXAGON

Draw a circle and a vertical line bisecting its centre. Next, with a 60° triangle, draw a line to both left and right of the centre line from the point where the vertical and circle lines meet. Now connect the ends of the verticals where they cross the circle and you have a hexagon.

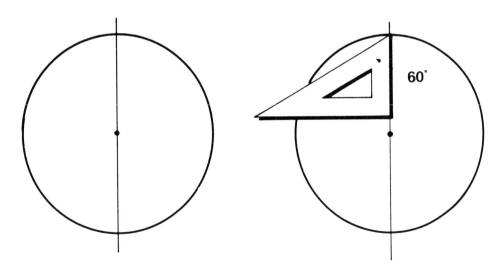

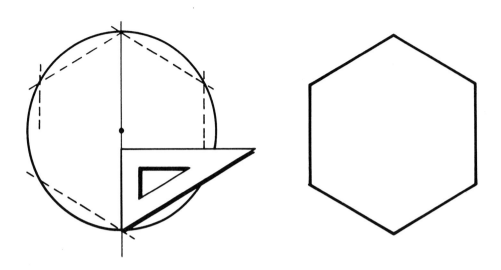

AN OCTAGON IN A TRICE

Draw a square and describe a circle inside it. Using a 45° triangle draw lines across each corner to complete.

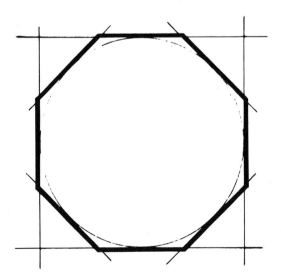

DIVIDING RECTANGLES INTO EQUAL PARTS

This technique is very useful for turning out evenly spaced columns if a page layout needs, for example, five columns. You may find that the type area comes out at an odd fraction that does not exist on any ruler. To solve this one, position a ruler at an angle across the page so that a number easily divisible by 5 aligns at the end. Tick off at regular intervals and then project your verticals up to cut the tick marks. This system works on any size and for any number of columns. It can also be applied in horizontal fashion, to break a line into equal spaces.

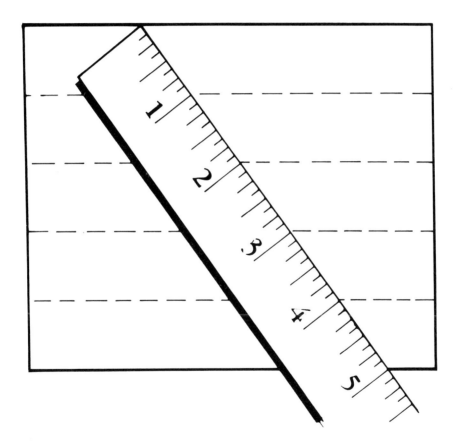

DIVIDING A CIRCLE INTO EQUAL PARTS

To divide a circle into a given number of parts, equal to each other both in area and perimeter, let the circle on A-B as diameter, be the given circle. In this case, it is divided into five equal parts.

Divide A-B into the same number of equal parts at the points 1, 2, 3 and 4. On A1, A2, A3 and A4, and on the upperside or underside of these lines, describe semicircles; then on B4, B3, B2 and B1, and on the upper or underside of these lines, describe semicircles running into the former ones, to complete the effect.

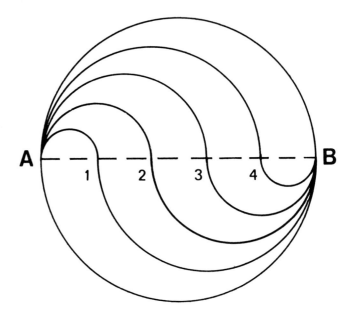

RADIUS CORNERS MADE EASY

Rounded or radius corners can be made more easily with the help of transfer lettering. Select a sans-serif C or an O and position it carefully in a corner of your pencilled guidelines, then scrape away the unwanted parts of the letter to allow the ruled lines to blend, as shown in the illustration.

The paste-up method is another useful way of achieving radius accuracy — not as quick, but better if the rules must be extra light. Set your ink compass to exactly the same width as the pen. (Use the pen from the compass if it is detachable.) Pencil in and ink the rectangle, carrying the lines away from the corners. Describe a neat ink circle on a piece of similar paper, with the radius corresponding to the size of corner you want. Cut the circle into four equal parts, and paste down each quarter

with rubber cement so that they mate up with the rules. You will now have four perfectly matched curved corners to the rectangle. This idea can be modified for any unequal area, providing the circle is cut in the right way.

Note: The quickest but by far the most difficult way of radiusing corners is the straightforward ruled-line method.

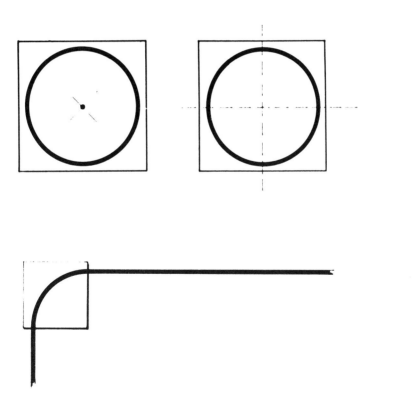

DRAWING AN ACCURATE 90° ANGLE

Draw a perpendicular line and place the point of a compass at the lower end of it. Next draw a semicircle to cross the perpendicular. Where the arc crosses the line, and without altering the compass, draw intersecting lines on the two sides of the semicircle. Use your straight edge to line up the two intersecting points, then draw a horizontal which will now be at exactly 90° to the perpendicular.

DRAWING AN ACCURATE 45° ANGLE

Draw a perpendicular and use the 90° angle method to draw a horizontal line. Take your compass next, and draw an arc linking the two arms of the cross. Where these two points intersect, use the compasses without altering them and describe two semicircles. Where these semicircles intersect, take the point furthest from the centre and link it with a straight line to the centre cross. The result will be an accurate 45° angle.

DRAWING MULTIPLE CURVES ON A LINE

If you want to draw a line that involves numerous curves, make a template out of card. Just trace the line on detail or tracing paper and paste it down on the card. Cut along the curves with a sharp knife and your template is complete. A length of clear tape laid underneath near the edge, will lift it slightly away from the working surface and help to stop ink-creep. Sandpaper the edge to smooth it if necessary, then burnish with a paint brush handle to toughen and round it off.

PARABOLIC CURVES

Divide a rectangle into equal number of spaces, then connect 1 to 1, 2 to 2, etc, as shown in the illustrations. Use a french curve to finish contours.

Layout and basic shapes

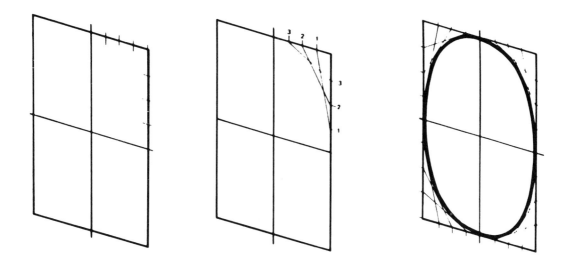

EQUALISING SHAPED OBJECTS

1. Draw a centre line and one side of the object.
2. Measure off required sizes from centre line to side with line across.
3. Transfer the measurements to the other side and connect dots.
4. Finally use french-curves, templates, etc to complete the shape and ink in.

FINDING THE HALFWAY POINT WITHOUT A RULER

If you ever need to find the halfway mark between two points without a ruler, simply take a sheet of paper and transfer the two points to the edge of the sheet. Next, bring the two sides together and fold so that the points meet. The exact centre will be where the creaseline occurs.

QUICK FIGURE-RENDERING

To make figure-rendering easy, search through old newspapers and magazines for suitable figures. Cut them out and position them under the top sheet of your layout pad, where they coincide with the layout. Sketch in the figure, altering and adjusting it as you work to suit your ideas. The result will be a slick, professional-looking figure that looks like the work of a specialist figure-artist. If necessary, the costume can be changed, whether it is a simple swimming costume or a formal ball gown. This method is far quicker than trying to sketch in the line detail straight away without any guide.

FOLDING AND CREASING

Packaging dummies — boxes, cartons, etc — can be creased neatly and professionally with the device illustrated. A wood block 10in x 8in in area and one inch thick, has a groove cut in it running along the top. The card is laid along the block-groove, lined up with the crease-marks. Care must be taken to ensure that the marks are accurate, otherwise the dummy will not assemble properly. Use your knife handle or a dried-up ball-point pen to score along a straight edge, so that a groove line is made. If it tears, you are either pressing too hard or holding the pen at too steep an angle, allowing it to dig into the card instead of creasing it.

50

INSTANT COLOUR CHECK

To save time mixing and testing different colours on dozens of mini-layouts, try using acetate colour sheets. These are obtainable at most art suppliers and cover a wide selection of colours, toned to approximate standard printing-ink colours. By placing a sheet lightly over your layout you will be able to see exactly what it would look like if printed in that colour. If you are trying to achieve a three-colour effect on a two-colour budget, place one sheet halfway over another, for example; magenta over cyan (pale blue) produces a third colour — purple. This technique is particularly useful in determining how photos will look when printed as duotones or halftones. Painting white or coloured line work on the sheet to check how reversals will look is another gambit, but more will spring to mind as you progress.

RENDERING DECKLE-EDGE EFFECTS

Use a steel ruler to strike the edges of the card lightly and at regularly spaced intervals. The effect is a fair imitation of the type of deckle used for special-occasion folders and greeting cards.

CONSTRUCTING A FIVE-POINT STAR

Divide a circle into four equal parts, A, B, C and D. Call the centre point E.

Now divide A-E in half to give point a, position your compass on this point, opening it up to C, and describe the arc C-b (b intersects line E-B).

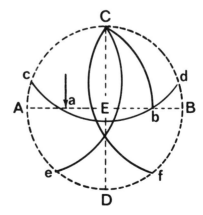

Now place your compass point on C, and extend it to b, describing the arc cbd as shown in illustration (right).

51

Layout and basic shapes

Position the compass point on c and extend
it to C, making the arc C-e; re-position it on
point d, extending the point to C and describe
C-f. To complete the star effect, merely
connect up C-e, C-f, c-d, and d-e, as depicted
in illustration (right).

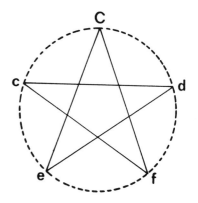

3: Mounting and presentation

SADDLE-STITCH MOCK UP

To make a realistic looking mock-up for booklet presentations, sketch out your pages as a double spread, to the approximate trim-size allowing 1in or so extra for subsequent trimming. The pages should be worked out as multiples of four, eg a 10in x 8in booklet becomes 20in x 16in in spread form. Make a crease down the centre of each spread, and gather them together to form the booklet. Now place them face down on a multi-sheet bed of blotting paper (newspapers or corrugated card will also do), taking care to keep the centre creases in direct alignment.

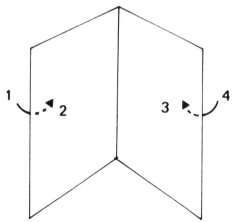

Open up a standard stapler so that only the ejector is used, and staple directly through the centre crease of the pages. Turn the pages over to check that the staple points have come through at the exact point of the crease, then press down each point to close the staple. To complete, merely trim the three sides to the correct dimensions and you have a booklet dummy that looks as if it was produced by a printer.

The size of staple used limits the amount of pages possible, so be sure to test your staples are long enough to pierce all the pages and fold back to grip the centre pages, or your mock-up will not hold together.

DRYMOUNTING TECHNIQUE

Drymounting can present problems when it comes to good adhesion of the print. Remember that both the mounting board and the material you are mounting contain a high percentage of water, which is natural in all paper. This must be removed before you can attempt any mounting, and it is done by keeping both mount and matter in the drymounting press for about ten seconds to remove the moisture by heat. Experience will tell you approximately how much time is required, as it depends on the thickness of board being used. Trim the drymounting tissue to the size of the work and with a tacking iron, fix the tissue on the back of your print at positions twelve, three, six and nine o'clock near the edges. Lay the print on the mounting board, and tack the corners to the mount, carefully avoiding creases. Replace both mount and print in the press and keep it under pressure for about ten seconds until the work is well and truly mounted. Providing you remove the water content of the board first you should encounter no difficulties, as it is the steam that causes poor adhesion.

MOUNTING ARTWORK

Matt-surface, self-adhesive film can be a big help in your art production, especially mounting. For dry-transfer lettering, simply letter directly on to the film with the words positioned at random. Next, carefully trim away each word with or without the backing. In the case of the latter, lay each piece of film with the lettered word on a sheet of siliconised paper so that they can be easily removed. By using a lightly drawn base-line, you can position each word accurately in the given area. To do this, carefully measure the total length of the words, minus spaces between them. Subtract this distance from the total pica measurement and divide by the number of spaces between the words. The resulting answer should be as accurate as possible and each word laid down with that measurement maintained.

54

Film can be used for illustration work by merely laying it down, including the protective backing, on to the finished drawing, and doing your finished pen-drawing by tracing. The film with backing is sufficiently translucent to see the master drawing underneath. Simply trim away your work, and it will adhere by itself in the desired position. Other uses for this film are: producing finished brush-script lettering from a pencilled original by overlaying the film, making a line drawing from a photograph; making a duplicate from existing copy; using it in conjunction with the artwork enlarger (camera lucida); or using it in the IBM typesetter for self-adhesive repros, etc.

You can also make your own colour areas, then position them so that they can adhere easily by pulling the protective backing away. A black area is easily produced by using a good opaque water colour, then cutting it to fit the desired area or to produce your own rules by the same process. On the black surface, white lettering can be applied for a good reverse. Yet another use for this clear film is in protecting finished work, especially dry-transfer lettering. It is easily mounted if care is taken. Where overlays are concerned, the film can be used with drawn or lettered work, and is mounted equally easily, with the advantage that work underneath can be seen through the overlay and film for spot register.

Alterations present few problems, as omissions can be added and errors scraped away. Where inks fail to take, simply use french-chalk powder.

MOUNTING LAYOUT PAPER

Due to the transparent nature of layout tissue, making a layout presentable via the usual sheet of dark cover paper can be difficult. Pasting the layout down flat on a sheet of white Kent is one solution, but this tends to impart a contrived look to the layout. One answer is to fold the sheet. Select a sheet about twice the size of the layout, fold it in half and pencil in the layout dimensions for guidance. Fold over the four sides until the sheet matches the layout size, either flush, or with a white border, as you wish. Tape the folds to secure, then mount the layout, gum only on the flaps.

The result is a neat professional-looking layout on pure white paper. With this method it is possible to do the layout either before or after the folding process.

MOUNTING A COCKLED PHOTOGRAPH

If you are supplied with a badly cockled photo to mount, apply rubber solution to the reverse of the print and the mounting board, Next, soak the print in clean water and place it in position on the mount. Use a squeegee or rubber roller to remove any surplus water and allow it to dry. The print will gradually shrink into a smooth surface as it dries. For thicker paper a quick method is to apply two strips of double-sided adhesive tape, one along the top of the layout, the other along the base.

DISPLAYING TRANSPARENCIES

Colour transparencies can be tricky things to present, as they depend on light passing through them to look their best. Naturally this makes it impossible for them to be mounted in the same way as a photographic print.

Mounting and presentation

The best way to tackle transparencies is to make a window folder as shown in the illustration. Select a sheet of four-sheet black card and fold it neatly in half. Arrange your transparencies in the most attractive manner possible to act as a guide for cutting the windows. Remember to make them slightly smaller than the transparency in order to conceal the colourless edges. Pencil out your guideline, then cut directly through the two sides in one smooth operation, and remove the pieces. Tape each transparency carefully in position with adhesive tape then close the folder and check to see if any are out of alignment before you glue or staple together the three unattached sides. The resulting professional-looking presentation allows the transparencies to be viewed in detail without the risk of clumsy handling. As a further protection, make a flap-type folder to wrap around the display; this will help to keep the transparencies free of dust or scratches.

COLOUR-SLIDE PRESENTATION

This method is useful for speculative presentations involving new business; or when the company advertising budget requires a boardroom decision. The procedure is straightforward, and consists of shooting and recording the relevant creative material so that slides can be made. The slides are loaded into the projector ready for the meeting, and any back-up matter such as copy or campaign proposals should be typed, photocopied, stapled together and placed on the table within easy reach of the executives involved.

Most presentations look better when blown up in size, but the visual effect of colour can add an even greater psychological impact to a presentation meeting.

RING-BINDER PRESENTATION

An effective and professional method of presenting artwork is to display it in a salesman's loose-leaf folio. Obtainable at most stationers, these hardcover books come in a variety of sizes and colours, and make a compact, easy-to-examine presentation piece.

The artwork is mounted on black or coloured filler sheets which fit into the transparent acetate envelopes of the book. The ring-binder principle permits the entire envelope and contents to be removed for replacing with fresh specimens when necessary.

PORTFOLIO PRESENTATION

Although normally used by artists seeking work in the art field, a well-stocked portfolio containing your best work can prove an invaluable asset when looking for new freelance assignments. Avoid the mistake of including too many specimens; a few selections of good quality are better than a large amount of inconsistent material. Include only your latest work as styles soon become dated — even to non-agency eyes — and work more than a year old may convey the impression that you are hard up for assignments.

To prepare finished art for presentation, choose a large sheet of medium to heavy cover paper, at least twice the size of the drawing including a border. Score a line down the centre of the paper by cutting lightly into it with a razor blade or scalpel. Turn it over and fold it along the scored line, which must be on the outside of the fold. Use a piece of scrap paper to avoid soiling the mount, and measure off an area equal in size to the artwork, leaving a border on the bottom, top and two sides. Cut out, and remove this area, making sure that you cut only the front of the mount. Open it up, position and secure the art to the inside face of the back of the mount with rubber solution or cellulose tape, check for centring, then fold the flap over to complete.

PAINTING ON CELLOPHANE

In package presentation, it is often desirable to wrap the dummy in cellophane, both to protect it and enhance its appearance. Cellophane is a tricky material to paint on unless you have the paint that is specially designed to counteract a tendency to cockle. If not, you could use acetate, which is harder to wrap, or stretch the cellophane in an old picture-frame to keep it taut while you paint your device or message. This is done by removing the canvas from an old painting, and then taping it around the frame in the same way as the canvas. By tightening the wedges until it is stretched like a drum you will produce a surface that will accept paint or ink with a minimum of cockle, and retain its original shape when dry.

Providing your layout of the dimensions is accurate, you should find this method far easier than trying to paint the pack in three-dimensional form.

4: Lettering

HOW TO USE A RULING STICK

A ruling stick is a device similar to the signwriter's mahlstick, and is probably the most useful tool that an artist can have. To make one for yourself, simply plane a narrow strip of wood to a size 12in long by 3/4in wide and about an1/8in thick. Sand it down to a smooth finish and polish to reduce the absorbency of the wood when ink and paint come into contact with it. In an emergency, an ordinary steel rule will act as a similar guiding device for the brush.

Use it exactly as the mahlstick: hold the rule stick steady with the left hand, while the right runs the ferrule of the brush along the upturned edge of the stick as shown in the illustrations. The fingers of the right hand control and guide the brush so that neat, slick lines can be quickly drawn without having to resort to a ruling pen. It sounds easy, but a certain amount of practice will be required. There are countless different ways of holding the ruling stick for drawing both horizontal and vertical lines, but as long as the left hand holds the stick firmly in place, and the right guides the brush stroke accurately and consistently, you will have no trouble.

The accompanying illustrations show the hand and finger positions favoured by the author.

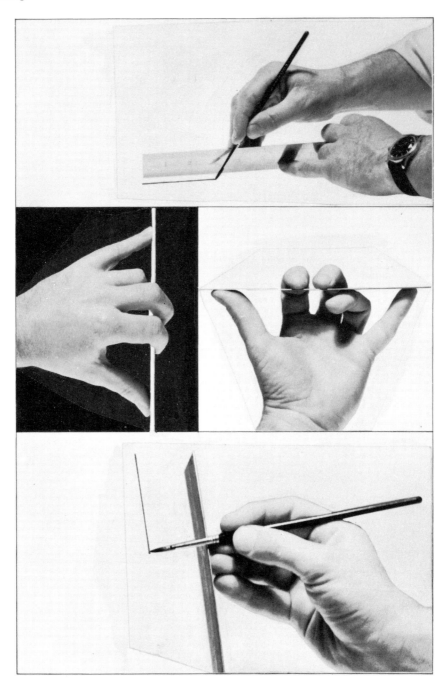

RENDERING EMBOSSED LETTERS

Embossed or die-stamped lettering is no problem if it is for reproduction. Produce black-and-white artwork as normal, choose a paper stock that lends itself to embossing, and the printer will do the rest.

If you have to render a blind emboss effect on a layout, paint the letters in white poster or gouache and keep going over them with successive coats until a relief effect is built up which simulates the emboss. It will take from four to six coats to build up the effect, depending on the consistency of the paint. Wash colour over the letters if you want to suggest die-stamping; if you also spray a little fixative over the letter, the resulting shine will produce a fairly close approximation. You may encounter 'flaking'. If this happens, add some gum arabic to the paint mix — it will act as a binding agent and help the relief letters stand up to rough handling.

Another method, popular in the greeting card industry, is to trace the design in reverse on to the back of your layout and place it face down on a bed of blotting paper (a dozen sheets is about right). Use the end of a paint brush or an old fountain-pen barrel to press the design into the blotting paper. Make sure that you burnish only the parts to be raised. Turn the layout over, and you have a realistic blind-emboss effect which can be coloured if necessary. This trick is ideal for the simple large area embosses, but impracticable for detailed lettering. Alternatively you can cut out your shape from fairly heavy paper (cartridge) and mount it down so it will not move. Next, place the layout paper over and burnish all over the cut-out until an emboss appears.

THE CUT-OUT LOOK

Draw out your lettering on tissue or tracing paper, then transfer-trace it to a white illustration board using blue chalk on the reverse of your trace.

Next, press down a sheet of transparent colour film (vermilion) but do not burnish as it should be free to be lifted. Using a razor blade or scalpel, carefully score, and cut out the lettering using the blue lines (which appear black under the vermilion film) as a guide. If you want a reverse or negative effect, remove the inside letters; if positive, burnish down the lettering and remove the background. Finally, clean off surplus chalk lines and touch up where necessary. The art is now ready for camera.

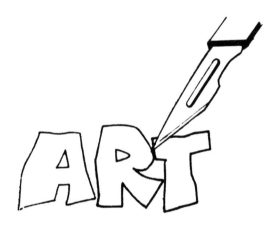

HOW TO 'AGE' LETTERING

The simplest way to get the 'time-worn' look to lettering is by retouching a normal type proof or a photoprint of type. You carefully dot the edges to produce the irregular, worn edge seen on the type in old books.

Another method is to use dry-transfer lettering. Burnish the lettering down well, then scrape quickly across the letters horizontally or vertically with a razor until you achieve a rugged, beaten effect. Clean up afterwards with a piece of solidified rubber solution.

LETTERING ON BLOTTING PAPER

Take a No 3 or 4 brush and a sheet of clean white blotting paper. Lightly pencil in the lettering if you need guide lines, or make a tracing first, and transfer it with a soft pencil.

Draw your lettering with quick, direct strokes, pausing slightly for the 'blob' effect to take. If you want more contrast between the lines and the blob serif effect, use a No 5½ pen, or thereabouts, and remember the quicker you draw the lettering the lighter it will appear; too slow and the ink will merge the letters into unintelligible hieroglyphics.

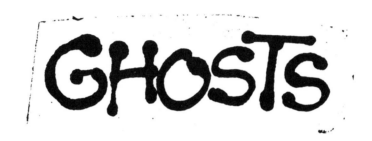

THE PERIOD HALF-PRINTED EFFECT

Choose a type-style that reflects the period required by the design; for example, Caslon is fine for the eighteenth or nineteenth century. Draw each character roughly but carefully with a fine pen, leaving a slightly textured look. You could also use dry-transfer lettering or repros. Use a brush with process white if corrections or further 'ageing' are required.

Another method, which results in a mottled, half-printed effect, is to cover a piece of paper with process white, then dab over the lettering until the best effect is obtained. Take care not to overload the paper with paint, and wait until it is tacky before dabbing the lettering.

Herald

FITTING TWO WORDS INTO A GIVEN AREA

Select your letter size for the given space, and position the first letter at the left-hand edge of your area, with the last letter of the right-hand word at the other edge. Start the lettering from either left or right. Naturally the right-hand word will be lettered from right to left (working backwards). If you have estimated well, the space between words should turn out correctly.

SPACING HAND LETTERING

These hints are about straightforward, optically spaced lettering. Gimmicks and typographical fads, like supertight spacing and 'stacking' of letters, are subject to current fashion and your ideas will need adjusting to suit.

The most common problem in lettering is how to fit a given number of words into a specified space. A safe way is to rough out the layout on tissue first. A little time

65

invested here will save doing it over again later. Determine the size you require and the number of lines the copy will take — a simple character-count will do from available reference. Next, use your judgement optically to space the letters evenly; avoid placing two upright forms, such as I's too close. Curved letters like O and C can almost touch.

Certain faces, like condensed sans, lend themselves to letter spacing more easily than other faces, as the illustrations show.

When you have a large amount of copy, be careful to avoid the 'rivers of white' spaces which will spoil the even tone or 'colour' of the type. If you watch the word and letter spacing carefully, you should be free from problems. A little effort at this stage is well repaid by the end result.

To simplify the problem of optical spacing, lay a piece of detail paper over your work so that it exaggerates the white spaces and shows up any uneven lines. Turning the work upsidedown is another good way to reveal spacing defects. Viewing the job through halfclosed eyes is yet another way; the type-matter merges, and shows up any irregularities in spacing. Do not forget the old lower case c method when you make a character count. This is the average width of letter for copy calculations.

Pale Ale

Pale Ale

PALE

PALE

66

ALIGNING REPRODUCTION PULLS

To paste up a repro pull or a strip of transfer lettering, use a straightedge to extend the baseline at the end of the strip, then draw a guideline on your finished art, so that the baseline on the strip will line up with it and you have no need to use a T-square when pasting up the lettering.

If it is difficult to see parallel baselines through a lettering sheet, the solution is simple, provided there are not too many lines involved. Take a sheet of paper and cut a slit with a very sharp knife along the intended baseline. Insert a piece of contrasting paper through the aperture, so that the cut edge will act as a baseline guide; this idea is particularly useful for the spacing of capital letters.

Care should be taken, however, not to burnish the whole of the letters down, only the top half above x-height (top line of the lower-case letters). This is because the letters C, G, U, O, Q and S slightly overlap the base-line when optically spaced. The descenders need even more care, or the letters may break up. When you have comple-ted the application of the lettering, all that is necessary to complete the job is to paste up the sheet, so that the cuts will automatically unite and eliminate the chore of having to retouch out baselines.

ALIGNING LETTERING

As each letter in a line is subject to the optical skill of the artist, it pays to simplify the process of alignment into mechanical accuracy by using the grid-line method. Take a sheet of graph paper and position your lettering, using the faint horizontal and vertical graph lines as your guide. The lines are printed blue and will not reproduce, so you have a permanent, horizontal and vertical line guide. A simple check before committing the lettering to the photographer or engraver is well worth while ordinarily, but with this method there is less risk of error. Dry-transfer lettering is particularly efficient for this trick.

ALIGNING DRY-TRANSFER LETTERING

An easy way to justify dry-transfer lettering is to begin by setting the longest word first, especially if there are only a few lines of copy which have to be justified on one word. Let us assume that word is 'character' – the other word/s will probably vary in length so you will have to choose a larger typeface to make a good fit. Let us assume that the other word is 'count'. Depending on the length of the words, a character-count method is advisable, so mark off each letter width on the edge of a piece of paper. Fix the piece of paper on the baseline, either above or below the first long word you have set, then set the line of lettering against the marked paper strip.

UTILISING OLD MAGAZINES

Search through your old trade or glossy magazines, until you find enough characters of reproducible lettering to make up a headline or a word. Paste up the cuttings in the normal way and retouch where necessary to complete.

ADAPTING DRY-TRANSFER LETTERING

If you ever run short of certain letters like Xs, Vs, Os, punctuation marks, or ampersands, try the office copier. You will get a perfect match to your lettering, provided that the copy is a good dense, black one. Burnish the characters on to a sheet of clean white paper, or use characters from the relevant catalogue sheet. Run the paper through the copier and you should get good, reproducible character duplicates ready for pasting up. Do not attempt to run the actual transfer sheet through the copier, as the polythene may distort the print.

FIXING DRY-TRANSFER LETTERING

As an alternative to spray-fixing, and depending on the scale of work, try using transparent self-adhesive film to cover lettering. It must be perfectly clear or it will lose sharpness in the reproduction.

CENTERING DRY-TRANSFER LETTERING

The simplest way to centre dry-transfer lettering is to lay out the lettering on a sheet first, then cut it up into strips. Draw a faint line through the strip to aid your eye, then duplicate it on your illustration board so that when you paste the strips in position, you will have a useful guideline to refer to.

REVERSING DRY-TRANSFER LETTERING IN AN EMERGENCY

Reversed lettering can be obtained by using ordinary black dry-transfer lettering on your layout provided that it is pre-released (burnished against the siliconised backing sheet partly to release the lettering). When it is pre-released, rub the lettering down on white or coloured paper and burnish it down.

Colour the area with a spirit felt-tip pen for preference, although water colour applied with a brush will also do. Make sure you cover the complete area, including lettering, and allow it to dry. Apply a coating of rubber solution (rubber cement) over the lettering; this will soften the printing ink sufficiently to allow removal with a piece of dried rubber cement.

Quite a good reverse can be made this way providing that the layout paper is not too soft textured.

PROBLEM SHOOTING WITH DRY-TRANSFER LETTERS

Rubber solution on the back of the paper may often affect dry-transfer lettering by acting as a solvent and bleeding through the paper. A simple remedy is to use either art-surfaced paper or imitation art to work on. The bleed-through of petroleum is minimised and you may find that lettering on a smooth surface will give an improved finish. Fixing will present few problems, providing you allow it to dry thoroughly.

DUPLICATING DRY-TRANSFER LETTERING

The only limit to the adaptations you can make with dry-transfer lettering is the style of typeface involved. For instance an O can be converted to Q or C. An H can be made with two I's joined with a centre bar. You do not even have to draw to complete the work – simply rub down a few printed guidelines from the lettering sheet and build up the finished letter. If you want to use only part of a letter – like the vertical stroke in the letter K – turn the sheet over, remove the backing sheet, and with a sharp knife cut through the printing-ink only. You can either scrape away the unwanted part or burnish down only the part required.

Some letters, whether upper or lower case, will double equally well. An obvious example will be the letter W, which in an emergency can be turned to form the letter M. Lower-case lettering will have more alternatives, such as: q for b and vice versa, two v's for a w, etc.

This trick is also useful for creating simple motif and letter symbols. Four folio U's for example will make a neat cross motif.

REMOVING DRY-TRANSFER LETTERING

Removal of dry-transfer lettering from artwork can be done in various ways depending on the size of the letter, the surface and its proximity to another letter. Use whichever of these methods you find appropriate.

Method 1 Scrape away the letter gently, using a sharp razor blade or knife, taking care not to dig too deeply into the board as it may cause problems in retouching or adding replacement lettering. This method will not work satisfactorily on cartridge or textured stock.

Method 2 Cover the offending letter with rubber solution (rubber cement), which softens the transfer letters and allows you to rub away the unwanted portion with dried rubber cement. This method is suitable for most surfaces but it is wise to mask off the other lettering in case of accidents.

Method 3 Press clear adhesive tape over the letter you want removed and burnish it down firmly. When you pull away the tape, the letter will adhere to its tacky side. If it does not come off at the first attempt, press down fresh tape and repeat the process until all traces of the lettering are removed. Here again, it is wise to mask off the other letters to avoid accidental removal of correct work. This method is unsuitable for rough-surfaced or bond-type paper.

FINISHED LETTERING AIDS

Black or white lettering is no problem, as all dry-transfer products come in those colours. However, if you want the same highly finished effect for your layout (in colour), use the ordinary standard dry-transfer lettering for the job in the following way. For dark backgrounds use white letters and position them on your layout. For light backgrounds, use the black lettering and burnish it well down. Next, wipe them over gently with a kneaded eraser (putty rubber), which helps to remove any grease.

Care should be taken not to fracture the letters in any way before the next stage. Paint over the lettering with the colour you want until it is all covered. The result will be a professionally sharp piece of lettering that will look as good as if it had been printed.

CHISEL LETTERING

If you do not have a one-stroke brush for 'chisel' lettering, an ordinary round type can be adapted in an emergency. Load the brush with reasonably thick poster paint and smooth it to the required chisel shape — it is now possible to squeeze the ferrule flat with a pair of pliers. When the paint is dry, trim the hairs with a razor blade and wash the paint out in water.

LETTERING VEHICLE DISPLAY PANELS

While sheer size is compelling, it also tends to exaggerate defects, which makes it important to get proportions and draughtmanship accurate. Here again, methods will vary depending on what and how much you have to letter. The simplest trick for ruling lettering baselines is to chalk a piece of string or stout cotton and stretch it along your intended baselines. Make sure that it is horizontally accurate by measuring and by an optical check. When it is positioned accurately, pull the centre of the string and let it snap into position again — the chalk will transfer and the result is a straight, easily removable chalk guideline.

The 'pounce' method goes a stage further. First draw out your lettering on a strip of paper (architects' detail paper is best) then prick holes in the outlines of

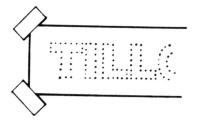

each letter. Some artmen prefer to do this by hand, which can be tedious; however there is a tool with a smooth toothed wheel which makes a neat perforation of the outlines. When you have completed this stage, tape the lettered strip in position on the surface and dust over the holes with a bag of 'Pounce' (powdered white french chalk in a cotton bag). The white chalk is ideal for dark backgrounds — for other colours, yellow is best.

The same principle can apply to roughing out white lettering on black showcards and display material.

SCALING GIANT LETTERING

First letter your work in large-size dry-transfer lettering, or by hand, making sure that the letter-spacing is correct. Now make calculations for each part of the lettering, ie if it is to be 10 (ten times larger), simply work from the base-line to the cap-height and multiply by 10. Then work along for each letter and space, multiplying by the size wanted. A second line can be drawn along the midway position between baseline and cap-height, to allow for curves in the letters O, Q, C, etc. For the letters S, P, and the figure 8, etc, draw lines to dissect the letters into four (halving the distance between the mid-baseline and base-line, and cap-height line).

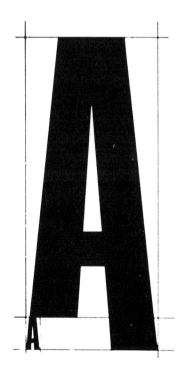

GIANT LETTERING

This is normally produced with a slide projector. Simply set up your lettering in type, photograph it, or make a dyeline master positive on film. The film is then projected on to a working surface (sheet of white paper) so that you can trace off your lettering, using the projected image as a guide. It is possible to save costs by lettering your own positive on film (dry-transfer lettering will do) and then placing the negative into the projector so that the film fits accurately.

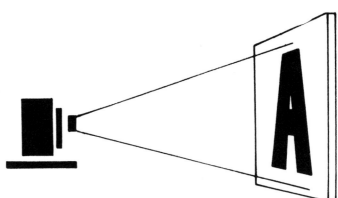

SUPER-QUICK LETTERING TECHNIQUE

If you have some lettering to do and cannot, for some reason, use dry-transfer lettering, try running a strip of clear tape along the cap-height line and baseline. (We will assume that you have already traced the lettering through with chalk or another tracing medium.) You then line in your letters with a ruling stick, allowing the vertical strokes to overrun the clear tape at top and bottom. When the paint is dry, simply peel away the tape to reveal sharp, clean-cut serifs to the top and bottom of each letter. The best results are achieved with oil-base paints on a glossy surface. Be sure to check that the tape is burnished well down or the paint may accidentally creep under and spoil the effect.

MASKING LETTERS FOR AIRBRUSH WORK

Draw the lettering in the normal way with a pencil, then mask it with clear tape along the edges. Cut away any areas that foul each letter, so that the lettering is open to receive the paint. When the spraying is complete, and properly dry, peel off the tape (it should come away in one piece) to reveal a neat line of lettering.

You can buy gummed Frisket paper (sheets specially designed for airbrush work), but you will find that transparent film, tracing paper or dry-mounting tissue are equally good. The non-adhesive papers mentioned need to be fixed with a coating of rubber solution. All trimming should be carried out with a new and very sharp blade. This trick has many applications as you will find with a little experiment.

LETTERING ON A CIRCLE

When lettering has to be spaced around a circle, project evenly spaced lines from the centre point to the circle line, and use them as centering axis for positioning each letter parallel to it.

TEXTURES ON AIRBRUSH LETTERING

Many interesting textures can be applied to the face of airbrush letterforms. Stipple effects are obtained by reducing the air pressure in the reservoir which results in a spatter effect. An even coarser, gritty look can be achieved with an old toothbrush. Simply load the bristles with fairly thick poster paint and flick the paint on to the lettering with a knife blade or your thumb.

LETTERING ON ICE

The most impossible tasks can often be solved quite simply. For example, to make lettering appear on a block of ice so that it looks genuine and not like type laid over a photographic print, simply set your words in dry transfer lettering on to a sheet of acetate, or alternatively, make a positive from type, position it on the ice and allow it to freeze in slightly, and merge into the ice until it looks natural enough to photograph.

DISTORTING LETTERS

Manipulating the negative in the enlarger is a good way to create special lettering effects, but a more reliable method is as follows. Lay out the lettering on white cartridge paper, or make a print if you have it already on negative. Take the print and bend it, fold it, crease it, screw it up, and in fact do whatever you find necessary to achieve the effect you want. (The floating-on-air look is achieved by heating paper until it cockles.) When you are ready, photograph the artwork in 'line' and record the image on negative for making bromide prints.

A distorted mirror is another effective if limited way of creating unusual letter-forms. The trick is to letter your message on white card and hold it in front of the mirror, so that the camera can photograph the image that the mirror distorts. A chromium-plated glazing drum is equally effective, and with a little imagination

other ideas will come to mind. Stat cameras and projectors like the Grant, Gateco, camera lucida and others, are ideal for distortion tricks. Enlarging and reducing is made simple, and by slanting the copy board many different perspective effects can be made.

DETERMINING THE CORRECT WIDTH OF SLOPING STROKES

For super-accuracy when measuring the diagonal or sloping part of a character, first get the width of the stroke on your compass, then place the compass point on one end of the line. Describe an arc, then repeat the process at the other end, and draw a straight line touching the outside of the two arcs. The resulting correct width will be a shade wider than the stroke shown by the dotted line.

PROJECTING 3-D LETTERING

Decide from which position the 'return' or thickness of the letter is to be viewed, then rule a 45° line from each corner to the desired thickness. To complete, taper off the two outside lines to improve the perspective effect. The dotted lines A and B indicate the original 45° angle.

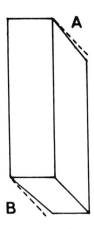
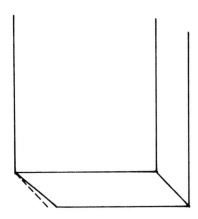

REVERSE LETTERING

The method used to reverse lettering depends on whether it is hand lettered, applied with Letraset instant lettering, or photographically produced.

The three basic methods described here can be adapted to suit the individual requirements of any reversal job.

Method 1 Letraset. This company produces a well-known range of ready-reversed (White) type. The only problem occurs when a large amount of reverse lettering is being done as in retail and department store advertising, when the difficulty of seeing guidelines through a polythene carrier sheet is most apparent.

solve this, try using a silver pencil (4B Stabilo) and you will find that the lines show up well. Keep them sharp to minimise retouching time, and avoid reproduction errors.

Method 2 Hand Drawn. Whilst an expensive way of reversing lettering, drawing it by hand is sometimes a faster solution than employing a photographer to do it for you. Outline each word in soft pencil on white illustration board. Next, all straights, both horizontal and vertical are ruled in. The curved portions are completed with a combination of compass and french-curve templates. The background is filled in, and any surplus pencil is cleaned off to complete the lettering.

This technique is particularly useful when applying tint patterns to 'grey' down letters (eg grey lettering on a black ground) and it eliminates the flaking which often occurs when white paint is used to draw over an inked-in background.

Method 3 Photographically produced reversals. Widely used in print production, photography is at its best when large, display size reverses are required. Whether you make your own negative, by applying black Letraset to a transparent cellophane film (for direct projection through an enlarger) or merely supply artwork and instructions to a process house, photography can do practically anything with lettering.

POINTS TO NOTE IN FORMAL SCRIPT LETTERING

Tilt your drawing paper to an angle of 25° to 30° from parallel, and you will find it is the natural position for writing italic letters. It enables the pen or brush to be kept at the normal position in relation to the body, thereby simplifying the lettering process.

To make a useful practice grid for script lettering, rule horizontal, mean and base-line guides in ink at about 25° to 30° on the board. Next add the ascending and descending lines, and you will have a permanent tracing guide which allows you to change sheets as often as you wish, without the chore of ruling in guide lines each time.

When it come to the actual letterforms, there are two basic pointers which must be observed. The first concerns the point at which the letters should be joined. The ideal place is about halfway between the meanline and the baseline. The second is the key to fluency in script lettering. When drawing the looped serifs in this face, avoid sharp upturns from the stem; imagine a small circle instead, and you will have a smoothly flowing line of script and not the spiky, hard-to-read version.

FORMING FREEHAND LETTERS

Practice for fluidity of stroke on the letter S; it is the best letter in the alphabet for this purpose. Using a standard one-stroke brush similar to that used by signwriters, it can be executed in three strokes. In block-letter form it ideally requires nine.

Drawing large-size letters can be great practice for developing a feel for lettering. The speed and dexterity of your stroke will improve greatly with time, and help you develop an eye for elegant, well-formed letters that will enable you to spot bad ones later.

Use the lettering-stick to produce the vertical strokes; you will find it an indispensable tool for freehand lettering.

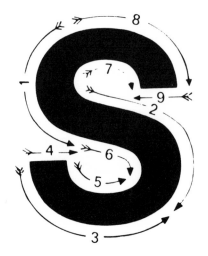

80

5: Trick photography

KEEPING A CHECK ON PHOTOGRAPHY

If you buy a large amount of photography on behalf of your clients, a good idea is to order reduced prints to paste in a file. Number each one on the back with a negative reference, the product name and any other relevant information. When you come to do future work these reference prints will be useful for comparing and reordering copies.

HANDLING PHOTOGRAPHS

A lot of problems can be avoided by the correct handling of photographic prints, negatives and transparencies. Never scribble on the back of photos with a ballpoint pen or any other hard instrument, the marks will show up in the form of crease lines on the emulsion side of the picture. Use a light felt-tip instead. Felt-tip pens are also ideal for writing instructions on the emulsion side of photographic proofs.

RETICULATION

This process produces a
granular, overall texture effect
that appears on the negative.
The image is broken into a
semi-abstract pattern which
looks like an enlarged mezzotint when printed. The
reticulation is obtained by
dipping the developed
negative into warm water
and allowing the emulsion,
to bring on the granulating
process. The print is then
permanently hardened in
cold water, and allowed to
dry. Many different patterns
can be made by varying
the water temperature and
immersion time on the
negatives, but it is a far
from precise trick, so it may
be necessary to try two or
three times before a satisfactory effect is achieved.

SOLARISATION

Exposing the negative to light during the development process and then developing
in the normal way will produce a solarised print. The picture may appear as a complete or modified outline, or when combined with black and white areas it can give an
illusion of ghostliness which is achieved by combining both negative and positive
effects in one print. It is also possible to reticulate a solarised negative to combine
the two effects. An illustration of a solarised print appears overleaf.

DISTORTION

The same principles mentioned in the section on lettering apply here. The feeling of depth in the line print was obtained directly — by tilting the copyboard or ground glass of the camera. The same trick can be applied to a continuous-tone picture by tilting both the negative and paper during exposure. There are special cameras on the market that incorporate an adjustable bellows which allows a similar distortion.

GROSS DISTORTION

This effect is obtained simply by using a fish-eye (180°) extreme wide-angle lens. The enormous depth of field of this lens distorts the perspective to an incredible degree, and the closer the lens is to the subject, the greater the distortion. It is a useful trick to make a 'stopper' or attention-getting picture, but the lenses are vastly expensive to buy, although it is possible to rent one from most large camera shops.

GHOSTING AS AN ILLUSTRATORS AID

Technical subjects such as engineering plant and equipment are best handled by using a photographic reference print, which is greyed-down or ghosted to about 50 per cent of its original value. The tone must be dark enough to see the detail clearly, but not so dark that it interferes with the inking. If you are using opaque poster-paint or an acrylic, there will be no problem.

THE MECHANICAL BLOW-UP TRICK

Complete your continuous-tone illustration, then get the process engraver to make a screened bromide print of your work. (100 to 120 screen should do, but it all depends on the size you want the final art to be, and whether you want a dot or a lined effect.) Copy the halftone bromide and blow the print up to three times larger. The result will be a bold, powerful-looking illustration that will reproduce perfectly in all processes.

PHOTOGRAMS

Interesting abstract shapes and patterns can be produced by laying objects directly on to photographic paper to make a negative image.

Under darkroom conditions, lay a sheet of clean glass over the photographic paper and position the objects on top. (The glass helps to keep the paper flat.) A few tests will quickly ascertain the best contrast of black, and once the print is satisfactory, the position of the lamp must not be moved or the exposure will be changed. The lamp should be about 3 feet away from the subject – and exposure time is usually about three seconds. Standard developer and fixing solution should be arranged, in that order, on the workbench, together with a rinse-dish of clean water. Ordinary domestic pie-dishes are ideal for containing the chemicals, and a homemade safelamp (so that you can see what you are doing) can be made by covering the shade of a household light with heavy brown paper. Be sure to leave an air-gap around the bulb so that the paper will not burn.

Providing all stray light is eliminated when you turn the light on, a warm yellow glow suitable for normal bromide paper will result.

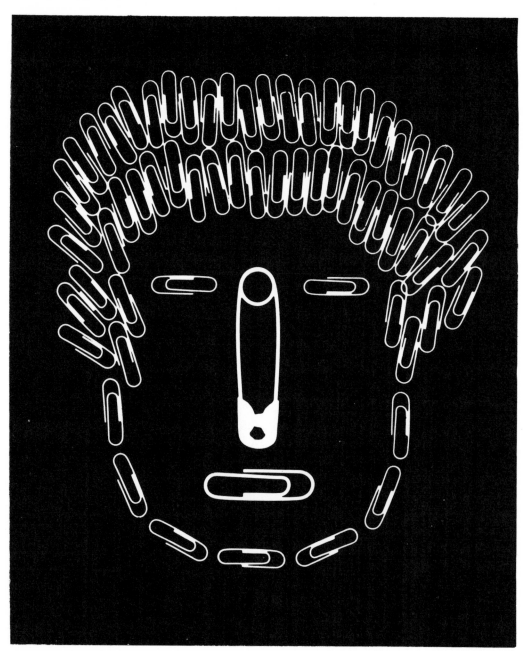

ILLUSTRATIONS FROM PHOTOGRAPHS

Obtain some clear film, and lay it on to the photograph; if necessary, fix it with tape. Using opaque white, paint all white and pale-grey areas carefully. When complete, you will have a piece of artwork suitable for fixing into position on a black background with reversed type etc. Also, you have a ready-made negative that can be inserted into an enlarger for producing prints.

THE CUT-OUT HALFTONE

The cut-out halftone or silhouette technique is fairly simple to any artist with a steady hand, but one or two points need watching. You will probably see photographs around that have been retouched in the unmounted state: this is bad, as it encourages cockling, curling and general mishandling. Make sure you mount the photo down on a generously thick board; this not only gives the photo a longer life, but minimises the flaking of the white paint. Ideally, the photo should be dry-mounted. If you want to do it yourself, practise on old prints first to familiarise yourself with the technique and materials involved. The alternative method is to mount it with rubber solution in the usual way.

If your print is glossy, it may need preparing before the painting-out commences, due to paint crawl on the glazed surface. A sure way is to use pounce powder obtainable at most commercial art stores. Sprinkle the powder over the entire print and spread it evenly with cottonwool. Remove it with cottonwool soaked in lighter-fuel so that the print has a slight 'tooth' or matt surface. The paint should now take readily, without crawling. It is possible to introduce a non-crawl ingredient into the paint, such as soap or a liquid detergent.

Any opaque white can be used for painting-out purposes, but be sure to mix the paint thoroughly before use. Place enough to complete the job in a mixing cup and add water. (Arrange it so that you do not have to mix up fresh paint in the middle of the job.) The correct consistency is something like fresh cream and is opaque enough to cover a black area in one quick stroke. Acrylic paint will help to prevent cracking, but it does not run as well as process white.

The outlining should be confined to the shape of the cut-out to be reproduced; it is unnecessary to paint out all the background. Paint around the subject as indicated in the illustration, using a pointed No 2 or 3 sable brush. Watch the paint to ensure that the consistency remains the same, and correct it if it shows any signs of thickening or thinning. Always paint up to the edge of the outlined shape, so that the bulk of the brush remains on the background area. To aid this technique, keep turning the work around so that the brush falls into place automatically. Use a ruling stick or ruling pen to paint in the straight outlines. They should be crisp and sharp and completed in one stroke if possible, rather than a series of jiggles. This one-stroke method avoids ragged work. If you make any mistakes, wash them off as quickly as possible with wet cottonwool wrapped round the end of a paint brush. Wipe it off with one clean sweep. It pays to rule in the straights before attempting the curves or tricky areas which will help you to avoid mistakes like painting out the wrong parts.

Each cut-out will have its own problems, particularly if it happens to be a badly taken photograph with an arm or a few fingers protruding from the general shape. In the latter case, it is often good policy to eliminate them completely without destroying the general effect, so that you achieve a line in the figure pose. Excessive clothing creases are often improved by 'tailoring', but take care that you do not overdo the painting-out and remove every single wrinkle, leaving a flat, woodenish-looking figure.

You may have a subject which is riddled with tiny inside areas like a car wheel's spokes or the tubes of some chemical plant. In that event, keep checking against a duplicate copy, or if necessary paint out the tricky areas first and the remaining parts afterwards.

When the whiting-out has been completed to an outline of roughly half an inch, trace off the shape, making your line a fraction inside the white outline, so that when you position the mask it will cover the unpainted areas. Now lay the traced-off area on to white cartridge paper and cut through both trace and mask simultaneously. Rubber solution can help to keep the trace in position while cutting. When the mask is finished, it can either be flapped into position or pasted down securely on to the mount.

CHEAPER HALFTONE ART

When the budget is tight, and the client requires a halftone block, photograph the original artwork and convert it to a halftone negative. Print it on photographic paper in positive form, ie a bromide print, and pass it on to the production department with an order for an inexpensive line block. The combined cost of the bromide print and the line block will normally underprice the cost of a straight halftone plate.

These line prints can be made in almost as many screens as halftone blocks, and if there are any problems with newspaper fill-in, it is possible to compensate by ordering an open-dot screen for your print.

The prints can be retouched by hand, highlights can be dropped out and the solids inked in to make combination line and tone illustrations. It is inadvisable to order exceptionally fine screens, but a word with your printer and process house will tell you exactly what degree of fineness you can go to. Newspapers and magazines usually require a standard screen size which should be verified with the periodical concerned.

BURNOUTS WITH A PHOTOCOPIER

The simplest way to pro-
duce a burnout is to run
the photograph through
a photographic copier
with the light setting at
'lighter'. This produces a
pale copy with most of
the main detail showing.
There are only a few
copiers around that pro-
duce an image black enough
for this process – the
Copycat and the Thermo-
fax machines are particularly
good. Working directly on
to the print, ink in any
missing detail and white-
out what you do not want,
run the work through the
copier once again so that
you get a good, crisp black
copy. Any pale tone should
automatically be removed
by the copier process, but
to safeguard this, paint out
any really dark areas not
required. Not all pictures
lend themselves to this
technique, trial and error
being the only sure way to
find out.

REALISTIC ART FROM PHOTOGRAPHS

Lay a sheet of frosted acetate over the photograph, and render the figure in whatever technique you like. This can be mounted and used as finished artwork. If you are using a magazine source as reference, watch the copyright regulations, but provided your trace constitutes new artwork in line, as opposed to the tone original, and you keep it anonymous, there should be no problems.

CLEARING AND REDUCING TONE PRINTS

The clearing and reducing of prints by chemical means is rarely done by top professional printers as it is usually unnecessary. There are times however (like in the vignetting process), when treating prints with chemicals can improve on results already obtained.

	Formula for Iodine-Cyanide Reducer		
A	Potassium iodide	¼oz or	6g
	Water, up to	10oz	250cc
	Iodine (flake)	20grams	1g
B	Potassium cyanide	40grams or	2g
	Water, up to	10oz	250cc

To use this reducer, make up to 20oz (500cc) with water from 1oz (25cc) each of A and B. It can be made stronger if required, depending on how much reducing you intend to do.

Handle Solution B with care as it is extremely poisonous.

To make a print with more contrast from a flat negative, give a slightly longer exposure than normal, and considerably more development in order to produce a dark print which is reduced with the iodine-cyanide solution. Local reduction is possible by applying the reducer with a brush or cottonwool. When the reduction process is complete, wash the print for about half an hour and dry.

VIGNETTING

To vignette a photographic enlargement means to fade-out the edges of the picture
so that it gradually decreases in tone to merge into the background of the print.
The soft but irregular edge is done by interposing between the lens a sheet of card-
board which has a hole cut into the shape of an oval or a circle; it can also be made
with serrated edges. The vignetting card is hand-held at about 4 in to 6 in from the
copy board, and either rotated or moved back and forth; the action should only be
slight. Certain subjects lend themselves to vignetting more than others, such as
portraits with light backgrounds. But with some clever blocking-out on the negative
it is possible to apply the vignette technique to great effect on subjects like product
shots and outdoor scenes. An alternative method of vignetting is by using chemicals.
The edges to be vignetted, or the background that is to be locally reduced, are cleaned
off by using an iodine-cyanide reducer as explained on page 91.

DEGREASING PHOTOPRINTS

A little methylated spirit on a pad of cotton wool will clean a photoprint of finger-marks or grease prior to retouching. As meths is a degreasant, any painting on the print afterwards will cause few problems.

CUTTING AND BUTTING

To butt or mortise two or more elements such as photographs, always position them so that there is a slight overlap either side of where the trim line occurs.

It is also helpful to make a tracing of the outline of each element to indicate their position and size. This is then taped to the board in the form of an overlay, and will act as a guide for pasting up the elements in their correct positions.

Prick each corner of the rectangles with a pin, or cut directly through the overlay and photographs simultaneously, so that you know you are keeping to the right boundaries of each print.

Lift up the edges with a scalpel or knife, and remove the surplus offcuts. The prints will then lie down to make an exact butt with no unevenness or sign of the join, other than that shown by the difference of the elements.

To complete, remove any excess petroleum gum, but be careful to rub only in the direction of the joins, or away from the edges. Failure to do this may result in a ragged edge and undo all the good work accomplished beforehand.

MASKING PHOTOGRAPHS

Cut out the aperture first, making sure that you do not overrun the corners, and position the mask on the (previously mounted) photograph. Use small pieces of adhesive tape to secure the mask to the mount, but take care not to press the tape down too hard.

This will hold it temporarily in place while you cut the top edge of the mask, about ¼in below the edge of the mount, to leave a small strip of mount showing. It is now only a matter of taping the mask to the mount. A 1 inch tape will cover both mask and mount and still leave enough to wrap over and around the back of the mount.

CUTTING PHOTOPRINTS

Although it is rarely advisable to cut a photoprint (it may be wanted again later) a good way to get positive results is by tracing the shape required on to detail paper and then mounting it on the print with rubber cement. Cut round the shape with a sharp knife or scalpel through both trace and photoprint, and remove the unwanted part. Peel away the trace before the rubber cement dries out and clean off the surplus with cottonwool. The cement tends to adhere to it which helps to clean the photoprint at the same time. This method will be particularly helpful in one-off display work where a random-shaped photograph, having no definite outline to follow with the blade, is to be mounted.

PASTING UP GIANT PHOTOPRINTS

Coat the mount with rubber cement and allow it to dry. Coat the back of the photo next, and lay a sheet of detail paper on it to delay the drying out. Position the print and pull away one edge of the detail paper to make adhesion. Pull away the paper gradually and allow the print to stick with hand pressure along the surface; this will exclude the air pockets and when completed a hand roller can be used to make firm adhesion. Note that the print should be coated with a thin film of gum only or it may pull away. This method will eliminate air bubbles and prevent the problem of accidental pre-adhesion.

BLEACH-OUT ILLUSTRATION

The photographic bleach-out trick is a valuable time-saver for speeding up work that requires great accuracy.

The method shown cuts out all preliminary pencil work and is far quicker than transfer tracing; it supplies the form and detail of the subject all ready for inking in, and is a great help in catalogue work.

Make a light print on smooth matt bromide paper; this is done by under-developing the print so that lightness is retained while the image can be easily removed later at the bleaching stage. The lighter the print is made the better, provided that the detail still shows up clearly.

Trick photography

Mount the print down, and remove any surface grease before commencing the inking process; the outline should be handled first, with the tones and shadows left until later. When all the ink lines and solids have been ruled in, examine the illustration carefully to check if any details have been missed before proceeding with the bleaching stage. (The bleach will remove everything except the pen work.)

The final step is to bleach away all the remaining tone. This is done with chemicals made up of iodine and cyanide solutions.

The formula is as follows:

The bleach-out solution

Two solutions are necessary and are as follows:

Solution A
Potassium iodide   1oz
Iodine   ½oz
Water   20oz

Solution B
Potassium cyanide   1oz
Water   20oz

Mix ten drops of solution A and B to 10oz of H_2O (water). Pour the iodide and cyanide solutions into a container to make a clear mixture and hold the print over a sink while the mixture is poured on. The photographic image will disappear in about one minute leaving only the inked-in parts. To complete, wash off the chemicals with running water and allow the surface to dry. Do not touch the surface until it is completely dry. The

ink will not wash off, but
may smear badly if rubbed.
When the print is dry,
complete any further
inking and add the re-
maining design elements
to complete. (Other form-
ulae include: bichloride of
mercury; potassium ferri-
cyanide and hypo; or
thiocarbonate and nitric
acid.)

BLEACHING PRINTS

To erase mistakes on photographic artwork, use a bleaching kit. It is ideal for removing type and cleaning up unwanted detail. Re-shooting the negative and the use of
white paint are rendered unnecessary.

THE FLEXICHROME PROCESS

This process allows artists and photographers to make full-colour prints and transparencies from negatives originally used for black-and-white photographs.

A copy negative is made from an original photograph, negative, colour transparency or illustration, and the flexichrome is made from this. The flexichrome is
hand-coloured with special dyes that absorb into the image regardless of the colour
of the original subject.

In this way, an air hostess's blue uniform could be changed to red, green, magenta
or any other colour desired.

In the case of black-and-white photographs, these are retouched, copied, and made
into full-colour flexichrome prints, used for all kinds of visual advertising.

RETOUCHING TECHNIQUES

Unwanted backgrounds can be removed from the negative by painting out with opaque water colour up to the line of the subject; the background will then print as pure white.

Alternatively, a background can be painted or sprayed with an airbrush directly on to the print. The result is then copied. Subjects with clean outlines are frequently treated by cutting out part of the print, then mounting it on a carefully selected background. Unique effects can be attained this way, although some additional handwork with a brush or spray-gun may be called for to complete the illusion.

REAR PROJECTION

This method is often used by advertising studios and consists of projecting a positive transparency from the farther side of the screen on to a translucent background. The effect is transmitted via an optical lantern. This subject is lit and shot in the normal manner, and appears as if it were actually in the surroundings of the projected view. Plain backgrounds can be turned into interesting scenes by expert retouching. This is done with a pencil and a sharp knife on matt surface film — the ideal medium for this technique.

CROPPING

If there are no individual print reductions involved, illustrate your cropping instructions with S/S (same-size) prints. If you use an office copier to make copies of original photographs you will save a lot of time and money, and at the same time provide an accurate proportional cropping-guide for the process engraver.

ADDING PATTERNS TO EXISTING NEGATIVES

Providing your negative has reversed portions, eg. the lettering, it is a simple matter to apply some zip-a-tone or Letratone tint to the back of the negative for printing in the normal way.

The example shown here was the easy way out when it became necessary to adjust a product symbol to suit a different range. Positive diagonal lines were applied to the reversed-out broiler symbol with the result shown.

SHOOTING FOOD

Photographing food can bring its own unique problems. For instance, what can you do to prevent ice cream from melting in the hot studio lighting? and how do you make bubbles appear to order on soup? The main task of the food photographer is to make the picture look as realistic and appetising as possible. He has to resort to various tricks and substitute materials to get the right effect.

If the flavour has to be conveyed visually the photograph must show steam rising from a hot pie for example. But pies and other hot meals have a nasty habit of cooling down whilst the equipment is being set up; to beat this, use tobacco smoke or steam rising from a block of ice on which hot water has been poured. Ice cream melts exceptionally quickly under hot lamps: substitute creamed potato and you will be able to take as much time as you want on the shot. If you have to create bubbles for a soup shot, add some washing-up liquid so that the bubbles will last long enough for you to make more than one exposure.

Keeping the head on a pint of beer is a difficult problem to solve. This is done by stirring either egg-white or sugar into the beer. Adding gloss to food can be another useful trick; smoked salmon for instance looks better when painted with glycerine, and cheese and butter are also more photogenic when given this treatment.

SAVING MONEY ON NEGATIVES

If you have to produce a regular flow of small illustrations, product symbols or logotypes, etc, try to hold some back if time permits, so that you can group six or more elements together for a one-shot, one-negative cost.

Proportional scaling is not important because each illustration will be used separately and at different times. The illustration shows the content of one grouped negative which was used for the author's series of paperback books, and which covered four different pages.

DWARF FIGURE EFFECT

Where you want miniature figures against a product for effect, photograph your model in the pose required and obtain prints. Mount the prints on card, cutting them out to the right size so that they are rigid. Position them on or around the product to be photographed and photograph the set. If you take care how you arrange them, a very successful illusion of 3-D will result.

FIGURE IN A BOTTLE TRICK

The trick is to have the base or back of the bottle removed. This is best done by a glass-cutting expert. Place the reduced photographic print inside the bottle, first having cut it out and mounted it for rigidity. The cut base of the bottle should not be too apparent, and can be retouched if necessary. The shadows will be completely natural if care is taken.

SHOOTING REFLECTIVE MATERIAL

Photographing highly reflective surfaces like silver and chromium requires careful handling. To reveal shape and ornamental detail, the lighting angles must be correct, and bombarding the subject with light from all directions is useless, as it merely renders many of the surface forms invisible. A study into the way light behaves when beamed on to a highly polished surface will prove very profitable for the photographer specialising in this field.

There are, however, various tricks which help to achieve dramatic effects, ranging from light tents to reflector cards. A light tent over the subject helps to hold a shadow 'edge' outline which is vital when shooting against a light background. The same problem arises in a different way with dark backgrounds. To avoid shadows merging into the background darkness, use white reflector cards. Time spent on the careful alignment of lighting and reflector cards will be amply repaid at the print-making stage. A useful trick for enhancing the gleam of silver is to place the subject on a dark polished surface, so that its reflections are extended on to adjacent areas. Retaining the gleam on chromium and silver is far easier when the subject is placed against a dark background.

Trick photography

When (according to the law of optics) a job appears to be virtually unphoto-graphable, use reflector cards to light the areas that are giving you problems. They will naturally appear in your picture but you can remove them from the final print by clever masking and some inspired print-making.

GOOD
Here the silver effect was achieved, by making a voile light tent to shield the cup from the glare of the lights, cut unwanted reflections to a minimum, and generally

avoid the ugly shadows that appear in the bad example below. An alternative, widely used method of achieving the same object, is to spray the silver with an aerosol matt dulling-spray. These sprays are obtainable at all professional photographic suppliers.

BAD

The harsh and clashing reflections on this example are a direct result of uncontrolled lighting. The studio lights are clearly shown in the reflection on the side of the cup, and various ugly shapes appear to distort the stem. Too much time was wasted in the attempt to get a highly polished look to the cup.

MIRROR TRICKS

Many interesting creative ideas can be achieved with the intelligent use of a mirror. Products can be enhanced by varying the viewpoints and use of different lenses and camera techniques to create multiple-image effects.

HELIOLINOGRAPHY

Basically a line-conversion technique, the heliolinographic process converts tone photographs into contrasting line representations of the original. The effect is something like a mezzotint, and reproduces economically and well. Not all photographs produce good line conversions however, and until experience has been gained on many different subjects, it will be very difficult to assess the probable result without actually making a print.

To make a heliolinograph, you need a same-size continuous-tone copy negative from the original photogrpah. Next, by contact in a vacuum frame, make a continuous-tone film positive from the negative. Expose and develop it to the same density as the copy negative. Register the continuous-tone negative and positive accurately, then position them back-to-back in total register. This 'sandwich' is put into a whirling printing frame with a sheet of high-contrast litho film in contact with the positive. As the sandwich revolves in the frame, the film is exposed to a stationary light-source tilted at a 45° angle. The litho film is developed, fixed, washed and dried. Any retouching is done then. The heliolinograph is printed on high-contrast paper, or it can be exposed directly on to an offset plate for printing.

BAS-RELIEF EFFECT

This technique produces a flat print giving a very effective illusion of relief.

There are two methods; one of these depends on individual skill in preparing the lighting and subject matter. The second, and most widely used technique, involves making a positive transparency from the original negative. When the positive is dry, it is placed in contact with the negative, but slightly out of register. The combined negative and positive are placed in the enlarger to make the print.

103

Trick photography

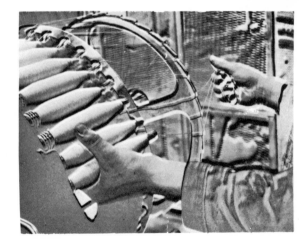

PERSPECTIVE SHOTS

The camera can be an indispensable tool for simplifying problematical line drawings. Cylindrical objects like cans, bottles or tubes can be shot in the correct perspective angle required, to provide an accurate tracing source. If in addition there is a complicated label on the product, cut it out and mount it in position on you artwork. Virtually anything can be photographed in perspective for line reproduction.

OBTAINING A SMOOTH BACKDROP

The easiest way of obtaining a smooth, shadow-free background to studio shots is to drape cartridge paper from a reel down a wall, so that it curls away at the skirting board. You can adjust the lighting to form a graduated tone of shadow from white, or direct the illumination so that it is a shadowless background.

PROJECTING AN IMAGE ONTO FORMS

This technique can give interesting effects, especially if lettering is projected on to a figure or shape. The projected image is then photographed in the usual way.

ANOTHER WAY OF USING REVERSAL FILM

To give an abstract effect to your work, you could consider using reversal film negatives as positives for reproduction. The colours will appear as the complementary ones to those photographed, ie purple daffodils, green pillar-box, orange sky, etc.

THE POLAROID CAMERA

This well-known camera, while often denounced as an expensive gimmick, can be extremely useful to the ad artist. It can make original art-copy for small items like logos or product packs, record visual evidence of displays, posters, vehicle livery, check colour renderings of models for fashion work, shoot package dummies for guard books and reference files, and make comprehensive layouts. The possibilities are endless. To make comprehensives, shoot the pictures first and have copy prints made up to size for pasting-up with the type and the other elements. A stat is made from this comprehensive so that the completed print has a slick highly finished look, suitable for clients who are unable to visualize from a rough. Shooting outdoor location pictures suitable for television commercials is another function of the Polaroid, it can render lightning visuals to which typelines are added directly on to print. The photogenic quality of advertising models can be instantly checked together with the studio lighting conditions.

PATTERNS AND TEXTURES AS A BACKGROUND TO A PRINT

The effect of a pattern or texture superimposed on a normal print is quite easy to achieve. First make a trace of the enlarged image of one negative for position, and do the same with the second negative. Say for instance that you want to produce a simulated, crinkled map without having to crease the map and spoil it. Shoot the line work on a line negative, then shoot crinkled paper on continuous-tone negative. Expose the line negative first and follow that by exposing the tone negative on the same paper. You will then have a good crinkled map effect. It is also possible to place two negatives together in the enlarger for certain subjects.

CONTINUOUS TONE IMAGE ON LETTERING

Either hand-letter your message on to carrier film, or apply specially prepared line-negative lettering. Make the exposure on to photographic paper, first ensuring that a trace is made of the lettering for position. Do not develop the print at this stage. The undeveloped image will be white on black. The next stage is to expose the desired area of continuous-tone image, then develop the print. You will then have lettering with a tone image. The alternative is to place the negative of lettering with the tone negative in the enlarger as one, so that only lettering with tone image is produced. In this way, a white background is obtained, because the negative image of lettering obliterates everything but the letter forms.

MONTAGE WORK

This method saves the trouble of 'burning-in' during the exposure of negatives – eg adding sky. By using many photoprints (with light in the same direction) of different subjects, scenes can be produced where location shots are not economical – for example, a tropical beach scene. A print of the beach is produced and tropical palms, figures, boats and ships, etc, are pasted into position and rephotographed. Any shadows cast by the paste-up must be removed. Any handwork should be carried out with an airbrush, and darks strengthened to overcome any loss in rephotography. The burning-in method simply means exposing a second negative of sky, for example, on a print that is uninteresting for lack of it. Some difficulty will be experienced in trying to make a montage of a sky where there are trees against cloudless areas. The intricate cutting-away of branches of a tree is not worth the trouble involved, and burning-in is the easiest way to overcome the problem.

MULTIPLE IMAGES

To produce the effect of movement in a static subject like a fist, simply shoot the image as normal. Next, project the negative on to the photographic paper in stages of exposure – moving the paper and exposing it the desired number of times. The background to the subject should, of course, be white in order that it is not exposed when printing. When developed, the print should give the illusion of high-speed movement.

Another way of producing this effect is to divide the overall camera exposure time by the number of images required – eg if the overall exposure time is one minute at f11, and four images are wanted, this will equal fifteen seconds at f11 for each shot. Care should be taken not to move the camera accidently while resetting it – a plate camera with a lens cap will overcome this problem. By this method it is possible to photograph yourself lighting your own cigarette!

SMOKE EFFECTS

During the exposure of printing paper, blow tobacco smoke across the surface. With practice and control, plus a little experiment, many interesting abstract and surrealistic effects can be obtained.

CHEAP LINE-CONVERSIONS

In all line-conversion jobs, some subjects lend themselves more readily than others. A photograph that has a strong outline like cranes against a cloudless sky would be no problem.

The cheapest method of making a line-conversion is by using a high-contrast photocopier like the Copycat. Provided you are not too worried about lack of certain tone detail or fine paper grain, you will get quite good results this way. Correcting loss of detail and whiting-out undesirable areas can be done when the print is dry.

UFO EFFECT BY DISTORTION

First obtain some high-gloss-surface acetate film and form it into a concave shape over a background scene with sky, etc. Stand an ordinary 60in lamp with a shiny, metallic shade so that it is reflected in the acetate when switched on. The reflection will be eliptical and glowing, superimposed on the background photograph. Any unwanted reflections can be removed by covering the causes of reflections with black paper or material.

THE CHILLED LOOK ON GLASSWARE

If you have to achieve this effect without a freezer or in extreme heat conditions, use an airbrush to direct cold water in a fine spray on the glass. Shoot your picture before the condensation gets out of hand and too many runs form on the surface.

TRICKS WITH COLOUR FILM

An interesting effect can be achieved by shooting artificial light film in daylight. This lends a blue cast to the transparency. Conversely, a soft red cast is made by shooting daylight film under artificial lighting conditions. Building interiors can look warm and glowing without being excessively red.

You can also make interesting effects using film of the reversal type and copying on to positive transparency by projection or contact methods.

Other colour effects should be obtained by using coloured illumination — for instance by photographing under red or blue lighting conditions.

LINE CONVERSIONS FROM COLOUR TRANSPARENCIES

It is possible to make very
good black-and-white line
conversions directly from
colour transparencies by
making a black-and-white
print from the transparency
and then copying the print.
This produces a black-and-
white negative which can be
be projected through a
screen in the normal way;
the results are often as
good as if the negative was
an original.

PROPPING UP STILL-LIFE OBJECTS

Occasionally you may have the task of shooting still-life objects so that they appear
to be self-supporting or floating in mid-air. Various devices can be used to achieve
this as illustration i. shows. The steel tubes were suspended with nylon thread from

a camera boom, while the drills were kept upright by embedding them in plasticine (children's modelling clay). A normal colour shot was taken and a transparency made. The nylon thread and plasticine were later cropped off and retouched to achieve the effect shown in illustration ii. Many other props can be used, but it is wise to check first with a retoucher to avoid any unnecessary expense.

PHOTOGRAPHIC FILTERS

Here are a few useful facts about coloured filters in photography. Technically speaking, filters for light reduce the effect of wavelengths by absorbing them completely or partially. Light filters, then, are layers that do not scatter the light but absorb and transmit it. A filter that absorbs blue will appear yellow — the complementary colour. A filter that absorbs red will be the complementary colour — blue-green.

Remember that the primary colours are red, yellow and blue; the complementary colour for red is yellow-blue; the complementary colour for yellow is red-blue, and the complementary colour for blue is red-yellow.

To check the type of filter to be used, remember the principle that a filter of the same colour will render the object very pale or white. A complementary colour will render the object darker.

A correcting filter is used to give colours in prints the same luminosity as the eye sees. An ultra-violet filter is used for this purpose, as it removes the ultra-violet and the amount of blue. Mountain scenery for instance, usually has a blue cast, and a filter is used to correct the blueness and the haze. This can also be achieved with a pale-yellow filter, and many degrees of the colour are manufactured according to requirements. Further correction can be obtained by decreasing the amount of red light to which the film is exposed: it is filtered out by using a fully correcting yellow-green filter.

To increase the contrast of a blue sky so that the cloud effect is pronounced, use a deep-yellow or red filter. It follows that similar colours photographed with the filters used in black-and-white work will be reduced or eliminated. For example, a red post-box photographed with a red filter will appear pale grey. You may therefore consider special creative work using filters when colour film is in the camera.

To copy paintings, full colour-correction is needed and certain special filters can help to eliminate the old varnish, which obliterates much of the detail; the same applies to copying documents when they are brown with age.

Colour correction for transparencies of certain manufacture can be achieved, but instead of the colour being absorbed, it will be recorded. A film with a pronounced reddish cast can be neutralised with the use of a pale-blue filter.

It should also be noted that the aperture will vary with the use of different filters, and a chart should be obtained for critical work.

If you intend to use an ultra-violet filter regularly, a good tip is to leave it on for the complete session, or until you want to use the camera without it. This way the lens is protected from dust and accidental damage. Keeping the filter on will not spoil your general photography, as it helps in most situations.

BURNING COLOUR SLIDES

Many weird and wonderful effects can be created by controlled burning of colour slides. The trick is to hold a candle or an ordinary safety match just close enough to melt the emulsion without actually setting it alight. The results are completely unpredictable, and tend to vary between each shot. When a satisfactory effect is achieved, project the result on to a screen and recopy in the normal way. The effects will range from exploding bubbles to a Dante's Inferno.

TWO-HEADED MONSTERS MADE EASY

A two-headed, dual-expression effect is fairly easy to achieve. Choose a dark background and light the subject with one spot or floodlight and make sure that only the face is illuminated so that there is no overspill on to the background. This will help produce the drama. Take two shots with the model in the same position, but with different expressions for each shot. Develop the film, then cut it carefully, reverse one section, and butt or slightly overlap it with the other so that they can print as one negative. The darkness of the background will help to lose the join and facilitate retouching. It is also possible to shoot two pictures on the same neg by lighting the model from different angles.

MAKING NEGATIVES FROM DRAWING FILM

If you use polyester film as a base for working, it is possible to type directly onto it to produce typewriter lettering of any size from S/S up. Simply put the handmade negative into the enlarger and make a reverse print. The print can be used as a direct art source, or as a master for tracing off different-sized copies.

Interesting effects can be made by producing your own negatives. Super-large type can be made by applying dry-transfer letters onto film; writing with a soft pencil produces 'blackboard' type lettering; you can draw illustrations for enlarged copy, then trace from the print direct on to drafting film for artwork, or use the finished prints as reversed white-on-black illustrations. A speedy way of producing reversed illustrations is to make contact prints from line work on drafting film.

ECONOMICAL SMALL BATCH DEVELOPING

Mix a small quantity of developer — about half a cupful — and with cottonwool swab it over the print to develop it. Use a sheet of glass as a mount for working on the print — a wet surface to the glass will make the back of the print adhere. The warmth of the hand will cause the developer to warm up sufficiently to develop the print.

In this manner, a fairly large quantity of prints will be developed from a small quantity of developer and the solution will not deteriorate in use.

PAN AND ORTHO FILMS

Pan (panchromatic) films are most widely used as they are the only kind that can register the whole spectrum of colours in shades from white to black (the name 'pan' meaning all). Ortho (orthochromatic) film is widely used in process work for its inability to register blue. Interesting results can be had from using ortho film for effects — sky becomes very pale, reds become darker. In a portrait, blue eyes would disappear and the skin tone would become darker, the lips showing very dark. Skin blemishes would also be pronounced.

INFRA-RED FILM

Highly dramatic effects can be achieved with this film, and atmospheric fog or hazy conditions are eliminated. Infra-red film can therefore penetrate otherwise impossible photographic conditions, owing to its ability to register heat emitted or reflected by an object. If an electric smoothing-iron is photographed when hot, a white glow will be registered. Interesting effects occur when foliage is photographed: it appears white owing to the reflection of the infra-red rays emitting from the sun. If the foliage is dead it shows up as black. A portrait photographed on this film (or if an infra-red filter is used with pan film) will show a white face with black hair.

113

6: *Typography and proof checking*

CURVING A LINE OF TYPE

When the layout calls for a curved line of type, there are four basic methods by which it can be done: typesetting; photosetting; hand-setting; or by cutting up repro.

The easiest and cheapest way is to do it by hand, using optically spaced dry-transfer lettering. If you have to curve a line of repro, apply rubber solution to both the mount and the back of the repro, and allow them to dry. Trim close to the type at top and bottom until you have a narrow strip. Using scissors or a sharp knife, cut along the spaces between the letters, not right to the top or bottom but leaving enough paper to keep the lettering attached. Cut from the top to make a downswing, and from the bottom for an upswing. Position your proof carefully and mount the first letter at the angle you want, with the succeeding letters following one at a time, bending each one at the cuts. Align them carefully and a neat flowing line of type will result. One word about tight spacing — this method is difficult if the setting is tightly spaced.

TYPE RENDERING

There are almost as many ways to render text matter as there are type faces and to attempt to show all of them would be both impossible and impractical. The styles illustrated below show some of the better-known examples and explain the logic behind the method.

1 Thick lines are ruled with a chisel pencil and should be a medium grey tone. These wide lines are sometimes used to indicate a sub-caption with the line broken into word lengths.

2 These lines are ruled with a chisel pencil using short strokes which produce a variation of tone in each line.

3 Single lines are ruled closer together than actual typeset to approximate the mass of type and area.

4 Double lines are ruled with a pointed pencil to approximate the point size of the type to be used.

5 Double lines are ruled
   with a pointed pencil
   using short strokes to
   produce variation of
   tone on each line.

6 Looped lines broken
   into word lengths are
   drawn between lightly
   indicated guide-lines.

When the text is to be set in lower case, some ascenders and descenders should be indicated. A more realistic effect will be produced if you can change the length of each paragraph and vary the width of word indications.

SHARPENING UP THE PENCIL LINES

Using a piece of paper as a mask, place it along the edges of the lines so that the rough ends protrude and can be rubbed away leaving slick, sharp-ended type lines. When both sides are complete, spray the layout with an aerosol fixative

DRYING WET REPRO

One of the perennial problems of the rush job is how to avoid smudging wet repro fresh from the typesetter. Lightly dust it with talcum powder or powdered french chalk to dry the ink, but take care not to over dust as it may cause the type to become grey and reproduce as such. It should be as black as possible.

116

REMOVING REPROS

Pour lighter fuel along a blade that is in contact with the edge of the repro. You will have more control and there will be less risk of spoiling the rest of the work.

CHECKING PROOFS

When it is your responsibility to OK a printed proof, you will find that the arrow has suddenly become your best friend. Whether you are indicating positional changes, sizes for reduction, a move of type or just a plain 'examine this', use the arrow to draw attention to the position required. When type or blocks have to be aligned with another page, this too should be indicated with a line drawn to the point. Circle all areas where bad register and faulty make-ready occur, non-print areas or where the impression is weak. Place a cross above anything doubtful, such as battered type or grease spots, and make sure you examine more than one proof sheet as they tend to vary quite a lot, and a mark appearing on one proof may be missing on the next.

CENTERING TYPE-PROOFS

To centre a piece of typesetting, fold the top and bottom of the repro gently to find the middle. You can then locate the folds on the centre line. Alternatively, take a scrap of paper with a straight edge, and indicate the total length of the line to be halved, with two marks. Now estimate the middle and put a mark on the paper and on the repro. Move the paper scrap so that the middle estimated mark locates with the outer mark, and note the difference between the two points. It is now a simple matter to place a centre mark accurately on the repro.

POSITIONING REVERSED TYPE

The normal way is to mount it in position on an overlay for reversal on colour work. It is possible, however, to letter directly on to artwork, but most production houses prefer the overlay system to differentiate between continuous-tone and line work. They have to be shot on separate film in the process house — one a halftone screened film, and the other a line film. When the reverse is out of a solid area there are few problems, but if the bulk of the background material is half-tone or four-colour process, it is advisable to pre-check the area in which the type will fall before deciding

117

on its final position. The easiest way of doing this is to paint a rough approximation of the type on clear acetate. When dry, place the acetate over the artwork, and you will see by moving it around where the most legible positions are. Keep this in mind when making your final decision, and look for areas of even tone rather than violent contrasts which tend to break up the readability.

FIXING TYPEWRITER ARTWORK

It is advisable to mask electric typewriter repro (ie IBM) from fixative, as it tends to affect the setting through solvent action. In case of chemical reaction, always test an unusual surface first.

PASTING-UP SMALL REPRO

The fiddly job of pasting up small settings such as single words and numerals can be made less arduous with the following trick: trim the typematter out with the usual razor blade or scalpel; then fix it with water-soluble gum (office type). The best method is to pour a little of the gum into a pallet or mixing dish. Take a small paint brush, and carefully paint the repro with gum; the positioning will be an easy matter, as it will take about a half-minute to dry. Once the pencil guide-lines are drawn, it is a simple matter to align your repros to them.

RE-SPACING REPRO

When type does not fit the layout space allowed, it will become necessary to adjust the spacing between lines so that it does.

This is done by 'opening up' (moving the lines further apart) or 'closing up' (moving them closer together).

The easiest and safest way to re-space type is as follows. First, mount the type-proof in the desired position, then use a scalpel to cut neatly between each line as shown in the illustrations. Thin the gum with lighter fuel, so that the pieces can be easily removed and manoeuvred into the chosen position. Use dividers to check the accuracy of the spacing, and as an additional guiding aid when adjusting the type strips with the knife. To pick up awkward pieces like the thin slivers of paper in the closing-up operation, use ordinary domestic tweezers.

118

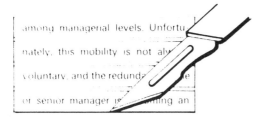

If word or letter spacing is necessary, use the same method as in line spacing, with the difference that the cuts are made between the words or letters. Take care to avoid cutting too deeply or ugly cut marks will appear on the artwork. To minimise this, use new blades straight out of the wrapper, or alternatively mount the type on a separate piece of Bristol so that the complete unit can be removed in one piece for positioning wherever desired. This trick is useful when artwork is subject to many adaptations.

RUNNING OUT OF REPRO

If you cannot complete a job because you have used up all available repro, check your typefounders' alphabet books; you may find a suitable type in the size and style you want. If so, run the page through a photo-copier (fluid type), and make as many copies as you need. Any cleaning up should be carried out on the print after mounting. The paper will paste up easily and is thin enough to avoid the deep 'steps' which sometimes cause shadows in the reproduction. The copies should be sharp and black, and printed on photographic paper, not thermal or electro-static copies.

SALVAGING WORDS

Some useful typesetting can be found in discarded leaflets and glossy magazines such as: 'Printed in England'; 'Printed in USA'; stock symbols, arrows or pointers, and decorative rules. All these may be salvaged and used, though they may need retouching. It is also advisable to have one or two stock art books containing copyright-free art and illustrations. *Graphics Ad Lib*, which supplies consumer art and ideas, and *Industrial Graphics Ad Lib*, which covers the industrial scene, are two highly useful sources of low cost artwork.

SALVAGING FOLIOS

When you need folios (printers' term for page numbers) and have no time to see your typesetter, why not use them from discarded glossy catalogues, if they are well printed?

CASTING-OFF BY THE LOWER-CASE C METHOD

A quick way to estimate copy in a given area is to treat every letter as a c in lower case. This is the average-width letter for lower-case lettering. Simply measure the width of the letter c and calculate the number of characters in the area, multiplying by the dimension of the c.

AVERAGING OUT LETTERS PER WORD

There are on average seven letters in each word of English written copy. To estimate the approximate number of characters in the copy, simply count all the words, and multiply the answer by seven.

LEADING BETWEEN LINES

Any doubts about leading and whether or not it will fit vertically, can be confirmed as follows. Remember that the next size up of typeface can be used as a guide, ie 10pt type plus 2pt leads would take up the same vertical space as copy set solid in 12pt type.

DIDOT AND PICA TYPE SYSTEMS

Remember that the Didot system has a larger-point body-size than Pica, and requires little if any leading. For example, 8pt on a 10pt body-size of Didot type equals 8pt pica type with a 2pt leading between lines. When specifying type, express the point size as if it were a mathematical fraction: 8pt on a 10pt body would be written as 8/10.

GROUPING TYPE

Illustrated below are examples of standard settings.

1 BLOCK FORMAT
Flush Paragraphs

The first explorers in Tibet were missionaries, searching for surviving remnants of the Nestorian Christian communities which flourished in Central Asia during the Middle Ages. In Tibet they found only

2 AS OPPOSITE WITH INDENTS

The first explorers in Tibet were missionaries, searching for surviving remnants of the Nestorian Christian communities which flourished in Central Asia during the Middle Ages. In Tibet they

3 CENTRED OR MIDLINE FORMAT

The first explorers in Tibet were missionaries, searching for surviving remnants of the Nestorian Christian communities which flourished in Central Asia during the Middle Ages. In Tibet they

4 MOBILE LINE OR GRAPHIC PATTERN

The
first explorers
in Tibet were the
missionaries, searching for
surviving remnants of
the Nestorian
Christian

5 VARIABLE COLUMN WIDTH
Useful device to enliven text
matter when practical

The first	surviving remnants
explorers	of the Nestorian
in Tibet	Christian commu-
were the	nities which flou-
mission-	rished in Central
aries, sea-	Asia during the
rching for	Middle Ages. In

6 FLUSH LEFT 'RAGGED' OR 'ROUGH' RIGHT

As in typewritten copy (unjustified)

The first explorers in Tibet
were missionaries, searching
for surviving remnants of the
Nestorian Christian communities which flourished in
Central Asia during the
Middle Ages. In Tibet they

ACCURATE TYPE-LINE MEASURING

For this method you need an enlarging and reducing calculator. Measure the length
of the first line of copy — say for example it is 5 inches. Note the 5 inches, and
count the characters on your type sheet that correspond with that length of line; if
we assume that it is 8pt type, then there will be 97 characters in a 30 picas or 5 inch
measure. On one side of the scale locate the inches (5) or 30 picas, and on the other
scale find 97 (the number of characters). Align these together, so that with the cursor you can determine the length of line according to the number of characters in
the given type-face. For example by moving the cursor to 19 characters, you can
immediately see that the length of line will measure approximately 1 inch or 6 picas.

122

This method makes accurate type-line length indications possible with little trouble, and if you use pica calculation throughout you can immediately see the number of characters there are in any given number of picas; taking the above example, there are in one em 3¼ characters, right up to any calculation you care to make. This is another use for the valuable enlargement and reduction calculator.

APPROXIMATING TYPE SIZE

A type size or space can be approximated without the help of lower-case alphabet tables or the square-inch word-count method. Rule off several square inches of a suitable type specimen, and count the words in the space to get a count per square inch. The typed copy will give you an idea of the total amount of words and an approximation of the number of square inches of space required for the chosen type. If your calculations are fairly close, send the type specimen to the typographer together with the copy and layout marked 'set to fit'.

Use of copyfitting tables is a better, more reliable method, and companies such as Monotype, Stephenson & Blake, or Mouldtype Ltd, produce tables to suit various typefaces and sizes.

COPY FITTING

To simplify the copyfitting process, manuscript copy for text matter should always be typewritten, double spaced, on 8 x 10in paper: left hand margin 1½ inches; right 1 inch; 1½ inches at top and 1 inch at bottom. This system leaves plenty of space for marking-up copy for type-sizes. A Pica typewriter gives 250 words to the page (8in x 10in), 60 characters to the line or approximately 10 words.

THE CHARACTER-COUNT METHOD

Count the characters in typewritten copy and compare these with type selected. Each space between words must be counted as though it were an additional character. Typewriting has 12 characters per inch if it is Elite, 10 characters to the inch if it is Pica, so that copy with 40 lines of Elite typewriting of an average width of 4in will contain 1,920 characters (4 x 12 x 40). You select the type you wish to use and if the layout provides a space 3in wide for type it is now a matter of counting the characters to the line.

The number of typewritten characters (1,920) is then divided by 36 (3 x 12) to get the number of lines of text it will take to carry the particular copy. The answer in this case is 54 ($53\frac{1}{3}$). The problem of horizontal space solved, attention is now turned to the vertical space. How deep will the 54 lines be? The answer to that depends on the type selected. This table indicates the number of lines to the vertical inch.

POINT SIZE	LINES TO THE INCH
4	18
5	14.4
6	12
7	10.28
8	9
9	9
10	7.2
11	6.54
12	6
14	5.14
18	4
24	3
36	2
48	1.5
72	1

Thus if type chosen is 12pt and the number of lines is 54, the space for the text will be 9in deep. If the layout permits only 8in for copy, either the art director or the copywriter has to give way. The above table is for type without leads — type with just the normal amount of spacing between lines. Add a 2pt lead between each line, and this must be taken into account when calculations are made. Therefore, 10pt type plus 2pt leads would occupy the same amount of vertical space as a copy block set solid in 12pt type.

TYPOGRAPHICAL ILLUSTRATION

Creating pictures with type is a fascinating if expensive exercise. There are many ways of handling a typographic illustration, as shown by the example overleaf, which is an interesting solution to what could have been a complex problem.

124

The brief required a
realistic-looking male head,
to be made solely with
numerals in order to give
a computer-age look to the
illustration. The solution
was to use an ordinary typewriter, so that by varying
pressure on the keys,
virtually a full range of tonal
values could be obtained —
something which would be
extremely difficult and
expensive to do via the
typesetters.

A photograph of the
subject was taken, and a
print made to a size com-
patible with the typewriter
face concerned. A sheet
of layout tissue was
rubber-cemented to the
photo, and the resulting
'sandwich' was placed in
the typewriter. The picture
was then carefully typed
out, working from top to
bottom and altering the pressure to render the subtle modelling of bone structure,
mouth and eyes etc.

Some numerals appear darker than others, for example an 8 is darker than a 1,
which is an additional aid in simulating tone graduation. When complete, remove the
tissue from the photo and mount it on illustration board for reproduction.

7: Illustration tricks

SCRAPERBOARD

Scraperboard is a china clay-coated board able to receive scraped lines, dots, etc, with a scraper tool. The heavy coating of china-clay makes it almost possible to gouge the surface. You can obtain either black-surfaced or white non-treated scraperboard and whichever you select will depend on the work involved. If there is a high percentage of black, then it will become obvious that black scraperboard should be used, although white scraperboard can be blackened with a wash of indian ink if necessary.

Original work is usually done twice or three times up on the reproduction size. It is not practical to work same-size owing to possible irregularities in the line, and it can be very difficult to control closely scraped lines anyway.

Scraper artists normally work from a black-and-white photograph, tracing the image down on mounted scraperboard for rigidity. Every detail is accurately drawn and the proposed tone lines are also drawn following the form. Where black lines appear on white, they are drawn in with a ruling-pen using a french-curve to round spheres, and straight lines, graduated to represent steel. The grain of wooden furniture is usually represented by black lines with gentle waves in them. Fabrics should represent as near as possible the original photograph, and regularity of pattern is vital, especially where folds and changes in form are indicated or else it will look

126

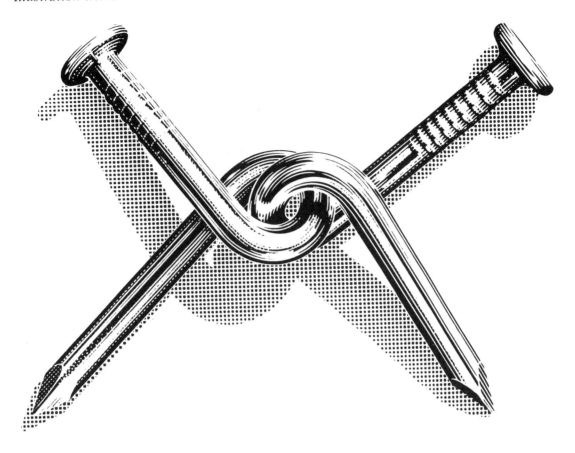

'sloppy'. The general rule to follow the form is best when in doubt.

The most indispensable tool the scraperboard specialist uses is a multiple-line graver. These are made in various widths and sizes which permit the artist to scratch up to ten lines at one stroke. They simplify cross-hatching, and if twisted during a stroke, alter the parallel width so that it produces a change in tonal value.

There are two basic methods of achieving a tonal effect which graduates from solid black to white. Method one consists of inking-in half the area, and drawing graduated lines to this area and scratching in the rest on the solid. Method two entails inking-in the whole area, and scratching out the horizontal lines graduating from a wide line to a thin.

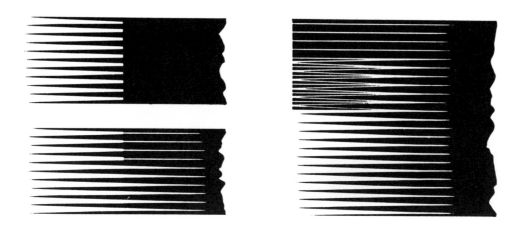

A curve or a cylindrical object will present no problems if the procedures mentioned before are followed. The difficulty of rendering regularly spaced, curved lines can be solved with the use of a french-curve.

The normal way of altering tone highlight variation is to vary the width of white

line. The wider the white swell in the line, the more the highlight is represented.

The techniques as applied to different forms such as cylinders, cones, cubes and spheres, etc, can vary greatly in execution. For a general guide, the lines should follow the shape of the form. Imagine a sliced boiled egg — the cuts follow the form. Likewise a head or sphere should have the lines following round the form to give additional three-dimensional effect.

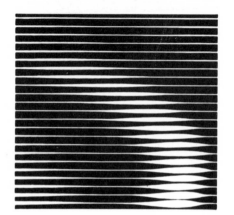 

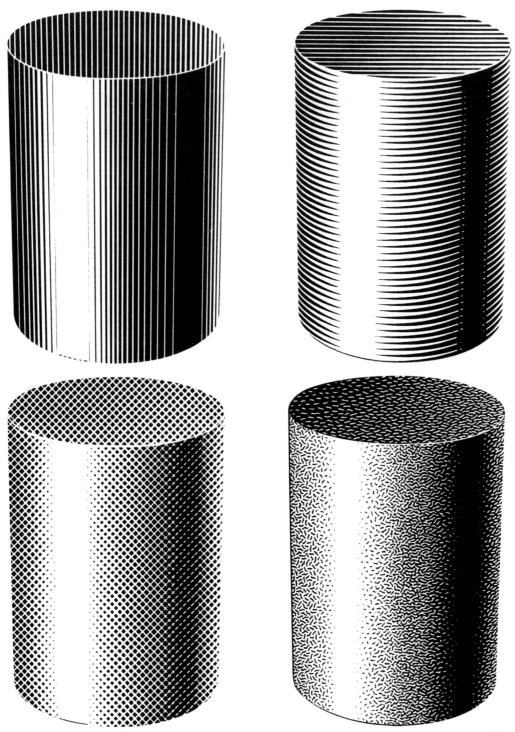

IMITATING SCRAPERBOARD

The scraperboard effect is achieved by the following method. Obtain a sheet of self-adhesive tint pattern (line preferably) and remove an area large enough to cover the drawing area. Lay this tint down on clear acetate or polyester film, and rub it down flat. Position this combination over the photograph and secure it with clear tape. At this point you will be able to see the image clearly through the film.

The next step is purely handwork — all you need to do is to scrape away the tint where you want the highlights to appear, and add paint or ink to solidify the dark areas. The mid-tones can be handled by the standard scraper technique of cross-hatching.

When the work is completed to your satisfaction, strip away the illustration from the photograph and mount for production in the normal way.

SELF POSING

For the front of your face and figure, a mirror is undoubtedly a help, though limited in its uses. If however, two mirrors are used, they can be angled so that your reflection in one mirror is seen in another. By adjusting the angles carefully, it is possible to get a wide variety of views of your own figure — back, side, or three-quarter. A trip to the local auctioneers' showrooms could yield a useful secondhand dressing-table mirror, which coupled with a hand mirror, would make an ideal reflecting device.

THREE-DIMENSIONAL ILLUSTRATION

Three-dimensional illustration can solve many a tricky creative problem and may be the best way to get a message across simply and forcefully.

Artwork constructed from children's plasticine modelling clay, thick acrylic paint, tissue paper and glue, fabric, wood, paper sculpture and other materials can often produce dramatic effects when photographed to the best advantage.

133

ILLUSTRATION BY CONTROLLED ACCIDENT

Sketch out your design lightly on illustration board, putting the colours (felt markers) where you want them to appear in the completed illustration.

Where black outlines or solid areas are to appear, leave white; the coloured portions are then completely covered over with white opaque poster paint.

Allow it to dry, then go over it again, this time with black indian ink. When this is dry, wash off the surplus paint and ink under the tap until the original drawing appears in colour with an interesting 'controlled loose form' look about it. The effect will vary each time it is done, and experiment is advisable before committing time and materials to the technique.

THE BANKNOTE LOOK

To give a parchment-like appearance to your art, first screw up the paper into a ball, then open it outward and spray with an airbrush from a low angle (30-40°). The lower the angle, the sharper the relief; when it is completely dry, flatten out the paper and mount. The result is a highly dramatic 3-D effect, suitable for subjects ranging from old banknotes to map contours.

THE MARBLE LOOK

Apply a mixture of different-coloured oil paint to an open dish of water, add a little turpentine, and lay a sheet of paper on the surface long enough to absorb the mixture. Remove it when a satisfactory effect is achieved, and allow it to dry with the colour face-up. This technique is used by printers to achieve the colourful whirl patterns seen on account books.

THE WEATHERED LOOK

Paint white lines of varying thicknesses over a solid dark background with the dry-brush technique and scrape it with a worn razor blade. This will achieve an 'old weathered' look as seen on ancient woodwork. With a little practice you will discover that it is possible to render virtually all types of wood this way.

THE MOTTLED LOOK

Smear some rubber solution on your paper or artboard, then use the back of a pen or brush to scribe lines and random patterns in the gum. When dry, paint over the area with paint or ink and again leave to dry. When the colour has dried, rub off the surplus gum.

TORN-EDGE EFFECTS

To get this type of effect, simply tear a sheet of paper (newsprint for coarse effect) to the shape wanted, and paste it down with rubber cement. Spray it with black, or paint it with opaque colour to cover the torn edge. Use cigarette lighter fuel to remove the pasted-down part and a clear torn edge will result. It is important that the surplus rubber cement is rubbed off carefully before you apply the paint.

136

ABSTRACT EFFECTS

Fold and crease a fairly thick sheet of paper, then apply a thickish blend of acrylic paint (different colours for each side) and press the sides together firmly. When the paper is pulled apart to dry various interesting patterns are created — some to order, if given careful guidance.

GRAVEL EFFECTS

For a rugged-looking texture, use a domestic candle and rub it lightly, or firmly over the surface, depending on how rugged you wish the texture to be. Next paint over the wax with a dry-brush technique. The result is a coarse gravelly-looking texture.

GENERAL TEXTURE EFFECTS

An interesting pattern can be achieved by putting paint or ink on to a sheet of plain or textured glass. If the glass is the plain window-type, you can get flat abstract effects, or alternatively you can increase the variety by using patterned glass; just press the paper on to the glass and a pattern will result. Adding a little frothy detergent can also help. A few attempts are necessary before you get a pleasing effect, but by adding different colours, interesting tonal forms can be made.

SHARP EDGES TO WASHES

To obtain sharp edges to background washes, use adhesive tape in the following way. Pencil in the guidelines and then lay strips of newspaper about ¼in away from the boundary. Next, lay the tape so that the edge of one half aligns with the area and the other sticks to the newspaper mask; then burnish. Now paint over the complete area with ink, watercolour, felt-tip pen or spray. It is then a simple matter to strip away the paper and tape in one piece, revealing a sharp edge to your area. This is the technique used by 'hand edge' painting exponents.

BRIGHTER PASTEL COLOURS

It is often difficult to keep pastel colour bright, as the tone gets muddier and darker when blended through rubbing into other colours. Colour can be restored by masking and spraying with numerous coats of fixative, scraping the pastel stick to make dust over the area and repeating the process many times in order to get the right tone. On no account rub the pastel after scraping, or it will diminish the recently achieved brightness.

MAKING A CRACKLE FINISH

Cover the required area with a flood of felt-tip marker ink (any colour will do) and leave to dry. When completely dry, go over the ink with an even layer of white poster or gouache paint.

When the paint is dry, paint over it with water-proof indian ink and wait for the crackle to appear. The technique is ideally suited for rendering a blistered paintwork effect.

138

CONTROLLING WASH DRAWINGS

The wash drawing or combined pen-and-wash technique is ideal for newspaper illustration when furniture or fashion is involved.

It is a difficult medium to control, but is capable of rendering beautiful effects when handled correctly.

The best approach is to build the illustration up with successive washes, keeping to selected portions to ensure complete control. A pencil drawing is made first, then transferred to the working surface. (A good-quality illustration board is usual.) Different textures give varied effects, so choose a board that will help you achieve the impression you want.

Next, apply a flat overall wash to cover the entire sketch, tackling the wood graining section by section, so that you do not have to make any rush decisions. Each area can be re-moistened as you come to it, so that the darker strokes can be introduced without any danger of the wash drying up too soon. Allow these dark strokes to 'feather', or 'bleed' in, to heighten the grain effect. Additional darker tones can be added later to accentuate any detail requiring it, and to increase contrast.

The next step is to rule in the outline edges to sharpen up the artwork, so that there is no danger of them being lost at the reproduction stage. Highlights can be painted in with opaque white, or scratched in with a razor blade, to complete the drawing.

CHALK TRANSFER

Take a single sheet of construction paper, and cover it with a thick layer of light-coloured chalk or pastel so that no paper shows through. Add a layer of crayon in a light tone over the chalk and ignore any dust that may be disturbed as a consequence. Turn the paper sideways and apply another layer of crayon, this time a dark colour. Now clip a piece of white tissue over the prepared sheet, and draw your picture with a dry ballpoint, a knitting needle or an H pencil. Unclip your paper to reveal the design on both chalked sheet and the white facing paper.

PATTERN TRANSFER

Pencil out your pattern on the surface you wish to transfer, for example, hardboard (the reverse side). When you are satisfied with the design, ink it in with a fully loaded brush and allow it to soak in just sufficiently to prevent it dripping during the impression. Turn the board over, and carefully press the inked surface on to your paper or illustration board, so that the texture reproduces. Allow to dry and retouch where necessary. Repeat the process for further copies.

139

DRAWING WITH GLUE

Try glue if you are after fresh and original effects. Glue can add depth to an illustration in the form of three dimensional textures, shadows and stripes. For example, a pop singer's hair, figures in the distance, or stripes on clothing, can all be picked out with long strips of glue to give a new impact to your work. Woodland and harvest scenes can be given an almost Van Gogh look.

There are many ways of applying the glue, from using a heavy paint-brush to squeezing directly from the tube. You can also press shapes into the glue for a repeat pattern. Experiment with different makes of glue until you find one you like. Colouring can be mixed in with the glue, or painted on when it is dry. Inks give a transparent look, opaque water colour will add a matt look.

140

TEXTURE WITH A TOOTHBRUSH

A really rugged-looking texture can be made by using an old toothbrush. Just dip
the bristles into ink or paint and flick along the bristles with your thumb or a knife-
blade, directing the spray carefully on to your mask. The paint should be fairly thick
in consistency so that the opacity of the dots will be constant.

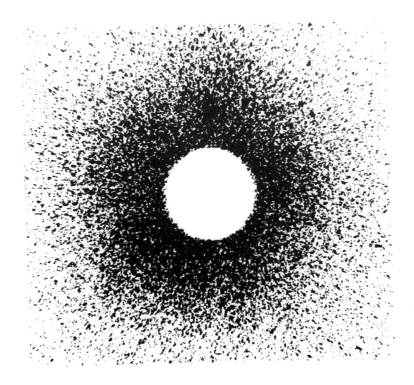

PATTERNED SILHOUETTES

Cut out any random illustration from magazines or newspapers, and paste the offcut
surround down with rubber cement. Clean away the surplus cement, and be sure that
the mask is well mounted. Next, use felt-tip markers to draw lines, dots, washes, etc,
so that they overlap to form other colours. Remove the mask with lighter fuel, and
the result will be a multi-colour silhouette effect

141

CREATING ABSTRACT PATTERNS

If you are looking for an interesting colour background to photograph, take two ordinary sheets of clear glass, about 4 feet square, and some coloured inks (the sort that have pen fillers in the caps). Place the sheets together one upon the other, and feed the colours in controlled quantities between the sheets. As they creep in and merge, you will see many beautiful and original design-forms created. Careful control of the ink flow and some slight tilting of the sheets will produce the colour proportioning desired. When the pattern is completed to a satisfactory state, shoot the picture directly through the glass. Do not part the sheets until you have finished or the design will collapse into a muddy neutral colour. This technique has obvious applications in home furnishing, textile and wallpaper industries.

PAINTING ON KROMECOTE

Kromecote and many other coated printing papers make an interesting surface for producing tone illustrations; the surface soaks up the paint almost instantaneously, giving an opposite effect to the merging washes obtainable on water colour paper.

The bubble effects often seen in today's colour illustrations are produced by adding a dash of soap to the paint. This trick is used in combination with the Kromecote technique.

THE BRASS-RUBBING TECHNIQUE

Make a rubbing with white wax crayon, taking care not to go over the edge of the brass. Pin the rubbing on your drawingboard and brush over the work with ebony stain. The stain will be resisted by the wax, allowing the original design to appear. When dry, crop the picture to fit the work, or to make an interesting room-decoration.

You can also make your own relief by drawing the design and cutting out sections for mounting. When mounting, leave a small gap between the segments, then make a rubbing in the usual way. This method can also be used for making emboss effects on layouts.

MAKING A FACSIMILE MEZZOTINT

The simplest way to render a mezzotint is to work directly from a photographic source.

Select a suitable picture, then trace off and transfer the areas you require. Next, ink-in the main lines, such as the outline of the subject. The areas that will appear as solids (shadows, etc) can be filled in to help key the layout of the illustration. Once the outline and solids are put in, it becomes a question of stippling-in the detail to approximate tone and architectural detail. The more you put in, the closer to a halftone it will become.

A crowquill nib is one of the best for this job, but an ordinary mapping pen works well.

8: *Finished artwork*

SQUARING A LARGE PIECE OF WORK

A large piece of work is often hard to square, due to the fact that it cannot be laid on a normal-size drawingboard. Remember that you can make a 90° angle by measuring one side of three units, one side four units, and the remaining angle five units of measure.

INSTANT ARROW POINTERS

Modified arrow-heads on finished work or dimensional drawings can easily be made by using sans-serif dry-transfer lettering V's, in either upper or lower case form. Some will have clipped points or the conventional pointed ends, depending on the typeface. Draw the indicator lines first, then add the V (it will be much easier to position it against the inked line). It is also easier to clean up the lines afterwards by scraping away unwanted ink.

144

PASTING UP REVERSE PRINTS

Blacken the cut edges of a photoprint before mounting, as it is much easier at that stage. If the prints are already mounted, use a crowquill pen — the slight scratch action of the nib against the edge of the print works better than a brush and helps the ink to seep under the print so that it eliminates the white edges. To blacken the edges before mounting, use an old paint brush to run along the edges, with the ferrule end acting as a support and the index finger as a guide; far more control can be achieved by this method, and with less risk of accidents.

DASH LINES

Drawing in dash lines can be an extremely boring and time wasting job, especially if you have to measure both dashes and spaces. If an effect will suffice, try this approach: draw a continuous line, then white out the spaces using your eye as the sole guide to continuity; complete one dash at each end of the line before starting as this helps to enhance the illusion of even spacing.

Handle a rectangle in the same way; complete the corners first and work from left to right. If you are not too particular about the sharpness of your dashes, you may try the freehand method which calls for a higher degree of control and makes it harder to produce an even line.

USING A TEMPLATE FOR REPEAT WORK

To ensure uniformity of size and shape when inking borders, brackets and curved devices, make a template out of 2-ply Bristol board. If the device has two equally shaped sides, as in brackets, make it for centre and end curves only. (It can be reversed for the other side.) The template is cut out with a scalpel or razor blade, and rough edges, if any, are smoothed down with fine glass-paper and by burnishing. Paste a piece of thin illustration board to both top and bottom of the template to prevent the ink from bleeding underneath during the ruling-in process.

PACKAGING POINTERS

With all its folds and creases, it is vital to ensure that packaging artwork is 100 per cent accurate. The following hints should help to achieve this.

Obtain a blueprint or laydown of the display or pack, to give exact dimensions and locations of cutting and creasing rules. Check the printer's preference for size and methods of separating colours. Include register marks and make sure they are finely drawn; the bleed overlap between colours should be about 1/32in, to allow for board stretch or misregister, and should be automatic when keylining, as the thickness of the keyline will constitute the overlap of the colours.

Whenever possible, consult the printer before preparing colour-halftone art, to find out how he prefers the artwork prepared. Reverse all lettering that is to appear white by making photoprints or with dry-transfer lettering.

Mark overlays to show where colours are positioned. All cutting and creasing lines should be indicated by drawing pale-blue lines; cutting lines should be continuous, creasing lines broken.

Either prepare working drawings in full colour, and leave the separations to be carried out by the process house, or draw the background in black and white with the halftone illustrations in full colour. They can be done on the same drawing or left separate for the printer to strip in.

APPLYING MECHANICAL TINTS

A mechanical tint is an indispensable illustration aid in the hands of creative workers. You could of course instruct your process house to lay the tint from a matched sample, making the area solid vermillion red for a negative tint or solid pale blue for a positive tint, using water colour accurately. But if the cost factor rules the job, laying tints yourself is the most economical way.

Beware of great reductions if you should be using a fine screen, or the dots will merge. When in doubt, make your work S/S (same-size).

The two main types of tints are the wax-backed (which is easy to apply) and the self-adhesive kinds, which need some care in use. The simplest way to apply the latter is as follows. Use a sheet of siliconised paper (from dry-transfer lettering) to lay your cut-out area of tint, but leave a small edge of tint protruding from the backing sheet and position this on your work. Press this edge to adhere and gently pull away the carrier sheet so that the tint adheres without air-pockets. Do not burnish down yet, as you will first have to cut away the unwanted parts with a sharp scalpel. When this is done, pull away the surplus and burnish the area with a suitable tool, using the carrier sheet as a barrier.

Remember not to cut too deeply, because the marks will have to be removed later or they will photograph. The surplus pieces can be used again if they are replaced on the backing sheet. Position the tint so that there is an even tone all over the work, without exaggerated white or black areas. This can be difficult, especially on a curve. Countless patterns can be created by overlapping but too much pattern will mesh and destroy an effect.

Never try to extend a tint unless you are certain that you can make an undetectable join; it is better to re-do the job with a fresh sheet rather than attempt to match the dots, as the smallest of joins will usually show up.

Elipses present little problem unless there is no keyline to cut on; you will have to use your ingenuity if that is the case and draw against an elipse template in pencil, then cut around the guideline carefully. A disc shape can be achieved by using a compass cutter as detailed in Chapter I.

THE PART-SCORED PASTE-UP

With this method, it is not necessary to sand the edges of a print to eliminate the 'step' which causes shadows. First score the area and use a sharp knife to scrape away the emulsion. Turn the print over and tear back an edge to the scored line and continue to tear away all the surround, peeling the paper towards the centre of the print. The result will be a wafer-thin edge all around the print that simplifies paste-up and cuts shadow pick-up to a minimum.

REMOVING PASTE-UP ELEMENTS

The lifting and removal of photoprints or type repros that have been mounted with rubber cement needs careful handling; lighter fuel simplifies this job by softening the cement and should be applied to the edges of repro with an old paint brush to prevent damage to the printing ink. Work the petrol around and under the edges, giving it time to soak in before attempting to lift.

FASTER BLOCKING-IN

A great time-saver for filling in large areas of solid is ruby photo-opaque tape. The technique is simple, and you avoid the tedium of waiting for ink or paint to dry. The solid area is first keylined with the strips of tape laid down so that each one slightly overlaps the other. The surplus tape is then cut and stripped away leaving a neat light-safe area that will reproduce as solid black.

For larger work, it is possible to buy ready-made sheets which are self-adhesive and specially designed to separate colour or fill in solid areas without the need for overlays.

EMERGENCY SEE-THROUGH PAPER

To save time and avoid transfer tracing, it is possible to make ordinary drawing paper transparent by using pure alcohol (methylated spirit). Position the original underneath the treated sheet and make your trace when it is dry. Use this sheet as finished art; it will take long enough to revert to its original form to allow you to complete the work and save yourself the trouble of tracing down.

EMERGENCY ART PRODUCTION

If two people are working on the same job (one may be working on the mechanical, and the other on illustrations), it may be difficult to work to scale owing to the time allowed. A quick way to overcome this is to have the illustrations photographed and positives made to fit areas required on the mechanical. The film is then taped into position so that all the scaling will have been done in the camera.

TRANSFERRING DIMENSIONS TO ARTWORK

One easy way is to prick holes through the trace to plot the outside area and major dimensions. You can later strengthen the small holes with pencil marks, and draw connecting lines with a pen without resorting to a pencil again.

COMBINED LINE/TONE ARTWORK

It is always better to separate the line work from the tone in your finished art as they have to be separated anyway in the process house. For black plates, simply paste down the photoprints into position and then produce your line work on an overlay film. For white reversals on photoprints or full-colour artwork, use a sheet of clear acetate fixed into position with clear tape, and apply white lettering by hand or with dry-transfer lettering.

KEYLINE FINISHED ARTWORK

Keylining is one of the safest and most accurate ways of producing finished art; with the elimination of overlays, the registration of each colour is dependent only on the keyline, so that distortion through overlay stretch cannot happen. The thickness of the keyline will be the amount each colour overlaps the other, reducing the chances of misregister to practically nil. The reversal of white out of colour is best handled by negative photoprints or white dry-transfer lettering.
Note: It is important that a full colour layout is sent with the work to the process house as a guide to separations.

GROUPING ARTWORK FOR BLOCKMAKING

Large items pasted up on one piece, say three or four grouped together, usually require $\frac{3}{8}$in minimum for separation to allow the metal cutter to clear each one without damage. If they must be closer, instruct the blockmaker to separate the negative.

GROUPING ARTWORK TO SCALE

When you send grouped artwork to the process house, remember it saves time and money if the items are in the same scale so that they can be reduced together. Another point to remember is that the distance between each item should never be less than $\frac{3}{8}$in (10mm) on reduction.

ARTWORK FOR REDUCTION

As most drawings are drawn up in size, then reduced for production, it pays to make sure that the line work will stand reducing without any 'breaking away'. A certain way of avoiding this is to do all your artwork S/S (same size) — as it will appear when printed; however, when the work is intricate it may not be practical to produce it S/S. The answer is to prepare your artwork half-up or more in size and make your linework heavy (half-up) to compensate for reduction. By using a Grant projector or a reducing glass you will be able to see what it will look like when reduced and to estimate how thick your lines need to be when half-up in proportion.

Never produce artwork more than five times its smallest reproduction size, as the majority of photographic and process houses cannot reduce to more than a ratio of six-to-one. The cameras cannot handle such a great reduction without making an inter-negative, which increases your costs.

DUPLICATING ARTWORK

Where there is more than one example of an illustration required, hours of time can be saved by copying the art photographically and producing duplicate prints for paste-up. If, for example, there are a number of switches or taps of a gas-stove to be illustrated, you can either make up the art from S/S prints or from consecutively reduced prints which allow for perspective effect. This saves tedious repeat drawing where accuracy and detail is important.

HANDLING OUTSIZE ARTWORK

If your artwork is going to extend beyond the limits of the drawing board, produce the outline work smaller so that it can be photo-copied and blown up to the required size for tracing off. An alternative is to use the slide-projection method, as detailed in Chapter 4.

FLAPPING FINISHED ARTWORK

Take a sheet of cover paper and thin white tissue (eg detail paper) large enough for the work and lay them on the cutting board, white tissue on the top. Next, lay the artwork face-down so that the top edge of the work is right way up — not upside down. The top edge will usually be widest, and this should be positioned about 2 inches below the top edge of the cover papers, which should be placed squarely together without overlap. Now take a sharp knife and make an approximate 45° angle cut from the corner of the artwork to the top edge of the cover papers, so that both sheets are cut together. This will form a flap, to be pasted down with office paste or glue, white flimsy paper first, then the cover paper. It simplifies matters if you press down the artwork while pasting to prevent it moving. Press down the flap, and with a steel straightedge, cut away the surplus paper.

ARTWORK FOR DIFFUSION-TRANSFER PLATEMAKING

Plates produced by diffusion-transfer (from a paper negative by light-diffusion) require artwork to be as opaque as possible, especially on the overlays, otherwise the light intensity will cause non-print areas which are hard to overcome, and a new plate would have to be made. Try using opaque black paint rather than ink for this work, as the ink may tend to thin out in the solids.

Another point to remember is that during the making of a diffusion plate, it is relatively simple to remove spots or any unwanted parts but impossible to add to what is already there.

BORDERS AND PATTERNS MADE EASY

When a decorative border or design motif is required, check through your spare dry-transfer lettering for Os, Vs, Cs, etc. Most letters can be formed into patterns and if a section is run through the photo-copier, you need not waste more lettering than necessary.

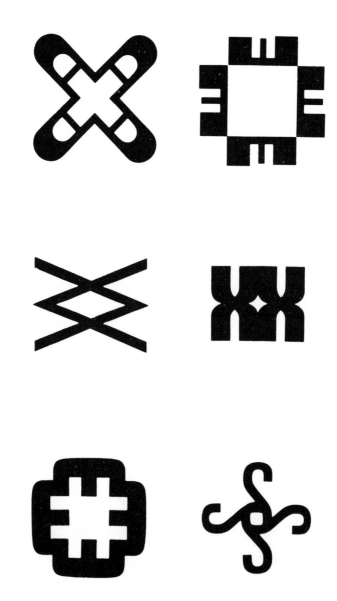

CLEANING AGED BOARD OR PAPER

When you have to clean a piece of white board or any paper that has become discoloured through age, use a little liquid bleach on a cottonwool swab round the end of a paint-brush handle and rub gently. Old newsprint engravings and book illustrations recover well after careful treatment.

FLATTENING CURLED PAPER

To flatten out drawing paper that has curled, cut two sheets of slightly larger paper, dampen them with clean water, and cover the curled paper back and front. Place this sandwich of paper under weights, or in a press and leave overnight if possible (depending on the thickness of paper). This can often help in an emergency where the paper is unmanageable.

ELIMINATING COMPASS HOLES

If you use a compass on finished art board to make a circle, the hole caused by the point should be filled with white. To avoid making a large hole in the art use a small piece of card, taped down in the centre before drawing the centre point. This piece of card is easily removed when the job is complete and filling in with white paint is unnecessary. An additional, faster way of concealing centre holes is by pressing down white self-adhesive stationery labels over them.

REGISTER MARKS ON MULTIPLE-OVERLAY WORK

If your artwork is going to require numerous overlays, it is better to confine the register marks to the board. Windows can then be cut in the acetate film of each overlay so that the marks show through when they lie perfectly flat. This will eliminate any inaccuracies in repeating the marks on each overlay.

REPEAT PATTERN PRODUCTION

You may be presented with an artwork problem where an overall repeat pattern is required, or where the design has a motif repeat, eg a Tudor rose. The most economical way to handle this is to complete one motif first, making photostat copies of as many prints as required to complete the design. To finish the job, trim and mount the prints in the correct sequence; this completed, the paste up itself can then be statted to repeat the number of finished patterns thus saving laborious duplication work. The normal method for pattern repeats is to obtain photographic prints for pasting up. The completed strip is then passed to a studio that has a step-and-repeat machine. This is by far the best way for the larger jobs where accuracy is vital.

SYMBOL SHORTCUTS

It sometimes pays to abbreviate artwork so that only half or part of the illustration is drawn. The completed part is then photo-copied and a reverse (left to right) print is made. This print is then butted up carefully with the original art to form a complete entity. The process can then be repeated to create duplicates or a decorative border as shown.

QUICKER INK RULES

A fast, reliable way to rule heavy ink lines is by using a needle-valve pen with a large-diameter nib.

If, for example, you are drawing a rule, merely draw a top and a bottom line and fill in the space between. The process can be speeded up by repeating the ruling to thicken up the guidelines. An alternative is to sketch a dense black felt-pen line so that it is larger all round than the required size. Pencil in your rule and cut it out with a knife for pasting in position on your artwork. Felt pens can also be used for filling in solid black areas; the ink dries quicker than the normal waterproof indian ink, and it photographs exactly the same.

It helps to keyline the outer limits of your area first with indian ink, so that the marker ink (which tends to be absorbent) does not bleed over the boundary of your keyline and create a fuzzy edge.

INTERSECTING COLOURED LINES

To avoid criss-cross lines spreading at the join, try using poster paint instead of ink. Ensure that the paint is diluted to a consistency that will permit a smooth, evenly flowing line.

If the job involves two colours, eg red and black, draw the black line first and the result will be a clean joint. If the red line is drawn first, the black will blob at the joint when it is drawn over it.

RULING EQUALLY SPACED LINES

A simple way to rule off equally spaced lines is by taping a ruler to the drawing board and projecting an equally spaced measurement such as inches. If you require the lines to be closer together than one inch, simply angle the ruler before taping in position — the more the rule is angled, the narrower the space between the rules will be.

A strip of double-sided tape will suffice to keep the ruler from moving.

AIRBRUSHING AN EVEN TONE

Care should be taken when airbrushing in flat areas and background tones. The best way to work is to spray even, horizontal strokes, keeping them as constant as possible with a slight overlap to each. The air pressure is controlled by the lever on the gun, which allows you to end the stroke with air only, and prevents droplets of colour from spattering the work.

When you need to convert a black background to white, you may have to spray many coats of paint with the result that paint dust forms on the surface. You can overcome this in a number of ways; one is to spray grey tones first so that you finish off with white, or spray some clean water over the dust so that the paint dissolves. Another way is gently to rub away the dust with a pad of cottonwool when the paint is absolutely dry.

AIRBRUSH COLOUR OR TONE MATCHING

This is best done by spraying the colour to be matched on clear acetate, so that when it is laid onto the work, an accurate match can be made. If you use paper to spray for matching, the whiteness can distract and prevent an accurate comparison.

Glossary

Acetate Clear material used for separations on artwork or covering layouts.

Actinic Light Light waves from the ultra-violet end of the spectrum. Special lamps are used to expose the printing plates, and a chemical reaction is made in the chemical coatings to form an image.

Advertising Agent A person or firm who accepts, on behalf of his client, the organisation and production of advertising.

Airbrush Spray gun like a large pencil used for applying paints, inks, etc, by air pressure through the nozzle from a compressor or footpump.

Align To line-up horizontally or vertically.

Ampersand 'And' abbreviated to '&'.

Appropriation A sum of money set aside for annual advertising expenses.

Art Director Co-ordinating head of a group of artists, designers and photographers with overall responsibility for the final look of advertising material.

Glossary

Art Paper Coated paper, the coating usually being china clay; it permits fine printing.

Artwork Any work finished, whether drawing, photograph or type-setting that is to be used for reproduction by a printing process.

Ascender Part of a lower-case letter, eg h, which projects above the x-height or mean-line.

Backing-Up Printing the reverse side of an already printed sheet.

Bank Standard heavy-duty stationery paper.

Bankers Flap A long envelope with the flap on the long side.

Base Line An imaginary line running along the base of capital letters.

Batter Refers to battered or cracked type with blunted or broken stems and serifs.

Bed Where the type rests when locked in the chase.

Ben-Day Material used for applying a mechanical tint of dots, lines or textures to a plate prior to etching.

Black-Letter A typeface derived from medieval script, eg Old English text.

Bleed Artwork that extends beyond the page area. To allow for bleed on S/S artwork, one-eighth of an inch is added.

Billing The total of advertising accounts that an agency handles.

Blow-Up A super enlargement of a photograph.

Blueprint A blockmakers' term for a photographic blueprint taken from the process negative prior to making a block. Any corrections or alterations can be made at this stage without block wastage.

Body Part of a piece of type between the back and the front of the stem or shank.

Body-Type text-matter of a book, magazine or advertisement.

Bold The name of a visual weight for type.

Bold Face Heavy letters used for headings to adverts, captions, etc.

Bond A standard paper suitable for letterheads.

Brainstorming A session where people concerned with originating a new idea get together and throw ideas about until a workable campaign solution is found.

Glossary

Brief A factual discourse relating to the product or service for which creative material has to be prepared, including sizes and format.

Broadside An unfolded sheet of any size.

Brochure A booklet bound and with stitches.

Camera Lucida A device which allows artwork to be projected, enlarged or reduced to aid tracing and proportioning. Three-dimensional objects can also be traced via the ground-glass screen.

Cap-Line An imaginary line running horizontally along the top of a line of capital letters.

Caps Upper case letters of the alphabet.

Caption Text for an illustration.

Caret-Mark The omission mark, used for instance on a proof to show where matter should be inserted. It is written in margin and text.

Casting-Off Chart A series of numbers corresponding to the numbers and sizes of characters in various measures to simplify calculation.

Cast-Off Estimating of the number of characters that are necessary to complete the area allowed for typesetting purposes

Character A single letter in a typeface.

Character Count The counting of each character to determine how many will fit in to a given area.

Chase A metal frame for locking-up type and blocks.

Clean-Proof Proof instruction to printer with signature meaning 'clean-proof required'. Specify number required.

Clean-Up To paint out, retouch, repair and generally clean-up artwork.

Cold Setting Type set by hand

Collate Gathering printed material into correct order of sequence

Colour Separation The separation of colours, either photographically or by means of overlays on artwork.

Combination A block or plate combining line and halftone process.

Compose Assembling type so that it will read and print as per layout and manuscript

Condensed Type Narrow letters with a vertical stress.

Contact Print A photographic print made by contact of negative with sensitised paper.

Continuous Tone A normal photograph or wash illustration.

Copy Text for book, advertisement, etc.

Copy Date Final date for copy, blocks, etc, to be at the printers or publishers of a journal.

Copy Fitting Calculating the amount of type required to fit a given area.

Copywriter A writer of advertisement copy.

Covers Usually two pieces of paper, one thin and white in contact with the artwork, and the other a cover paper to protect the work.

Craft Tint A liquid developer used to make halftone and doubletone effects when washed with different chemical solutions. The drawing is made on specially pre-pared board.

Cross-Hatching A technique in pen drawing to obtain a halftone effect.

Cut American term for printing block.

Deadline The latest time for delivery of work or the latest time for copy to be received by the printer.

Deep-Etched A plate or block with some halftone areas removed.

Demy A term for paper size (now obsolete).

Descender Part of a letter that descends below the baseline.

Didot The continental standard for type.

Die A plate used for embossed and relief work.

Diffusion Filter A filter used in photography to add effect to highlights and gene-rally soften the overall image.

Diffusion-Transfer Plate A litho plate produced without a process camera, but through a process developer. The negative is in the form of sensitised paper which reacts with the surface of the plate when processed through activating solution. The artwork must be same-size, as no enlargement or reduction can be made.

Dipthong A term used to describe two letters joined together, such as OE. This should not be confused with ligature, which is a term used for two or more lower-case letters joined together, for example ffi.

Direct Mail Printed literature sent through the postal service.

Doctor Blade The blade used on a gravure press for keeping the cells full of ink and removing the surplus.

Dot-for-Dot A litho method of reproducing a halftone original, using a screen in the process camera.

Double Impression This happens when two pages are transferred to the paper resulting in an effect similar to double vision.

Double Spread Two facing pages of an open book or magazine.

Dry Brush An illustration or lettering technique, where opaque paint is dragged rather than washed for effect.

Dryers: A paste or liquid medium added to printing ink to speed up the drying process.

Dry-Mount Mounting artwork or photographs on mounting board with shellac tissue by means of a hot press.

Duotone Sometimes termed Duplex; a two-colour printing, consisting of two half-tone blocks produced from a single black-and-white photograph.

Duplicate Two or more printing blocks produced from the original negative.

Dyeline A method of reproducing drawings and blueprints.

Egyptian A style of typeface with solid block serifs.

Electro Short for electrotype; a duplicate printing block produced from the original by means of a wax or lead mould on which copper is deposited by electrical means. The copper shell is then backed with metal.

Em The square of the body type (any size). Usually refers to 12pt, and is a standard unit of measurement.

Glossary

En A space equal to half the width of an em.

End Papers The blank pages at the beginning and end of a book. They are sometimes decorated with a pattern, or with artwork of some kind.

Engraving The general term for the making of a block by hand or process.

Esparto Paper made from esparto grass.

Etching The process of producing a printing surface on copper or zinc by acid etching.

Face The printing surface of type, plate, block, etc.

Fine-Line The treatment applied to line blocks required to show fine detail.

Flap Usually a piece of cartridge paper fixed on to artwork to act as a mask so that one piece of artwork can double for another size.

Flexographic A letterpress process using rubber plates.

Flock Printing A method of applying a felt-like material to achieve special effects.

Folios An alternative term for page numbers or pagination.

Format The layout, size and general specification of a leaflet, book, booklet, etc.

Forme Type and blocks, etc, locked up in the chase ready for the press or for duplication in the foundry.

Fount or Font The range of a typeface, including all punctuation marks, signs, numerals, etc.

Four-Colour Another term is full-colour; a reference to the number of plates (four) normally required for producing a colour picture (Yellow, Magenta, Cyan and Black).

Freelance Self-employed person who produces work for different organisations.

Frisket Paper A thin, transparent film-like paper used by retouchers and airbrush artists for masking of areas not required to be coloured.

Furniture A printers' term for strips of wood or metal spacers.

Gatefold A fold in printwork that opens like a double gate.

Glossary

Ghosting A method of reducing photograph contrast with frosted film or an airbrush filled with opaque white.

Gravure A method of printing called intaglio. The image is in the form of recesses or pits, and their depth determines the darkness of the image.

Greeking Indicating type on a layout, etc, by using simulated characters and lines as a substitute for text.

Grouped Work Items grouped together for blockmaking; however different their sizes, if items can be reduced by the same proportion, and subsequently separated into individual blocks, a considerable economy is made.

GSM Abbreviation for 'grammes per square metre'. A term referring to the weight of paper.

Gutter The centre of two pages in an open book.

Hairline Spacing Extremely thin spaces used for letter-spacing of type.

Halftone A printing block or plate made by photographing the original through a screen. The printed image is also termed 'halftone'.

Half-sized Paper which has received a small measure of sizing

Hard-sized Paper which has received a high measure of sizing

Hanging Par The first line of a paragraph projecting on the left.

Head The top margin of a book page.

Heading The title at the top of a page.

Heliolinography A photographic effect converting a continuous-tone photograph to line.

Hot-Press An off-white cartridge paper for drawing, finished by a hot press.

Hot-Setting Producing type by casting in molten metal.

House Organ A magazine produced by an organisation for internal circulation, as opposed to a magazine on sale to the general public.

163

Imitation Art Paper An economical substitute for coated art paper.

Imposition Laying out sheets to form pages in the correct sequence when folded.

Imprint The name and address of the printer or publisher on the title page or at the end of a book, or an agency's name on an advertisement

Indent Usually one, two, or three spaces (em quad) at the beginning of a line in a paragraph.

Initial Letter An ornamental or large capital.

Interlay Process where layers of paper are added between plate and mount to correct unevenness and add additional pressure where needed.

Interrogation Mark Proof correction term for ?

Intertype Name of the manufacturers, and also for the machine that sets type in lines or slugs.

IPH Abbreviation for 'impressions per hour'.

Italic Sloping type originated by Aldus Manutius.

Itals Abbreviation for italics, in copy instructions.

Jacket The design area of a book, formerly a dust cover.

Jobbing Printer A firm that produces general work of a small nature, such as stationery, etc.

Justify To set type so the left and right-hand margins form a straight edge down the page.

Keep Standing Keep type matter in readiness for a reprint.

Kern The part of type metal that overhangs the body, as in the letter f.

Keyline A method of indicating the position of colours to be used in colour printing. Can also refer to a coding system used to check advertisement response.

Kill Delete from copy or typesetting.

Latent Image An undeveloped image in the emulsion of a film.

Lay-Edge Sometimes also termed grip-edge, and to be allowed for when preparing print work. The part of the sheet that is gripped mechanically to be fed into the press.

Layout A blueprint to show where the art, photography, lettering and type will appear, and at the same time give an impression of what it will look like in print.

Lead A thin strip of metal manufactured in many point sizes for spacing outlines.

Letterpress A method of printing from raised images, such as type and blocks.

Letter Spacing Words extended by the insertion of spaces between letters: E X A M P L E.

Ligature Letters cast together to prevent kerns from breaking: fi; fl; ff.

Line Artwork Any artwork that does not contain a continuous-tone image.

Line Block A printing block without a halftone screen. A mechanical tint can be added to give a flat, grey effect but it will remain line block.

Line Conversion A black-and-white photograph with all middle tones eliminated or rendered in lines or dots by the use of screens

Linotype The name of a machine for setting type in a slug or line.

Logotype Trademark or namestyle symbol used by an organisation and abbreviated as 'logo'.

Lower Case The small letters of an alphabet, such as a, b, c, etc. It is indicated by lc.

Ludlow The name of a process for casting slugs from handset type.

Manilla A brown, heavy-duty paper mainly used for large envelopes.

Mat A window cut from a mat board to protect and improve the appearance of a piece of finished artwork.

Mats Matrices made from papier-maché. Stereos or stereotypes are made from this, cast in metal, and used for newspaper production by letterpress.

Measure The width of a line of type. Usually measured in ems.

Mechanicals Finished artwork involving overlays, separations, repros, assembly and paste-up, in other words, camera-ready artwork.

Glossary

Media The range of advertising outlets, ie magazines, newspapers, television, direct mail, packaging, point-of-sale and outdoor.

Monotype The name of a machine that automatically casts letters into lines.

Mounted flush Blocks mounted on wood or metal without the usual bevel-edge. The instructions given on the artwork are usually 'cut-flush this edge'. Flush blocks are useful where space is at a premium, as, for example, type can butt alongside the printing surface.

MS General abbreviation for manuscript.

Negative An image of the original black-and-white on film, used to produce printing plates

Negative tint A dark tint applied by the blockmaker or platemaker to a specific area. The artwork is painted with opaque vermilion as a guide to where the tint is to be laid.

Nickel-faced stereo A block cast with a facing of nickel to give it a longer life.

Nonpareil Six points or half an em.

Nut Printers' slang for an en

Old English Term used by printers in the early days for text or black-letter characters.

Overlay A sheet of transparent paper or film, taped to the artwork to act as a medium for separating colours.

Overmatter Type which is already set, but for which there is no space left in the forme.

Overprinting A blockmakers' term for type appearing with a halftone in black.

Overs The surplus of a print order to replace any accidentally damaged.

Orthochromatic A film that cannot record the blue end of the spectrum, abbreviated to ortho.

P Abbreviation for page. In plural, pp.

166

Paginations Numbering of pages.

Panchromatic A pan film is sensitive to the whole spectrum, and must not be exposed to any light.

Part-Work A series of weekly magazines on some particular subject that build into a library and permanent source of reference.

Paste-Up Term used for artwork involving the mounting and positioning of illustrations, photography and reproduction pulls.

ph value The degree of chemical purity

Photo-Distortion A method of obtaining creative lettering by distortion.

Photo-Setting The term used to describe typesetting by photography.

Photostat A photographic copy of an original, usually done economically by an office copying machine

Pica Unit of measurement in printing, equal to 12pts or one em.

Pierce To cut parts or windows in a block to permit the insertion of type.

Plastic Duplicates Halftones of plastic made from an original block. They are particularly useful for sending work overseas.

Plate A photo-engraving in metal, or the printing surface for a litho image.

Platen A small hand-press, either powered or operated by foot. Can also be the plate supporting the paper that comes into contact with the type.

Point The unit of measurement used in printing. It equals one seventy-second of an inch.

Point-of-Sale The point where advertising matter, in stores for example, is in visual contact with the buying public.

Points Marks in punctuation, or full stops.

Polyester Film A drawing film in various thicknesses which accepts pencil and ink. It is suitable for overlays because of its dimensional stability and resistance to petroleum and chemicals.

Positive Tint A pale tint applied by the blockmaker or platemaker to a specific area. The artwork is painted with a wash of transparent blue as a guide to where the tint is to be applied.

Posterization A form of double tone line conversion, can be done in colour or black and white

Pounce A container of powdered french chalk used by signwriters.

Press Proof instruction to printer with a signature meaning 'print off'.

Press Camera A large camera that accepts plates made of glass.

Process Colours Standard colours used in four-colour printing, usually printed in this order: yellow (chrome), red (magenta), blue (cyan), and black.

Process House A term used for manufacturers of printing blocks and plates

Progressives A sequence of colour pulls — one from each of four blocks, with a fifth combining all four colours.

Pro'ing-Up Scaling up for proportional enlargement or reduction.

Public Relations The dissemination of knowledge to sectors of industry and commerce.

Pull Rough printing proof.

Quads Pieces of type-metal supplied with the fount to fill out a line, ie a short line at the end of a paragraph or to centre a line of type.

Quoins Wedges of wood or metal for locking up typematter in a chase. The metal kind are made to expand by turning a key.

Recto The right-hand pages of books.

Reflex camera A camera with the view-finder so arranged that the subject can be seen through the lens.

Register The butting up of different colours of printing inks accurately. It can be loose register or hairline register.

Reglet Strips of wood larger than leads used for spacing between lines.

Reproduction proofs Reproduction pulls from typematter used for paste-up purposes.

Re-Screening Screening a screened original once more, for better reproduction.

Retouching The improvement of a photographic original by airbrush or by paintbrush. Retouching can be done directly on to negatives, transparencies or colour prints.

Reverse Instruction to the blockmaker or platemaker to reverse white to black, black to white, or left to right etc.

Revise Proof correction instruction with signature meaning 'submit another proof'.

Roman Normal upright typefaces, ie non-italic.

Rotogravure Also gravure, which is term given to a method of printing

Rough Term given to preliminary creative work which acts as a rough blueprint for an advertisement or leaflet layout.

Routing The method of removing unwanted parts of a printing block.

RP Printers' mark for 'reprint'

Rubber Solution American term for petroleum gum (cow).

Rubricated matter A paragraph or sentence printed red.

Running Head A title appearing on consecutive pages of a book.

Sans Serif Any typeface without a serif.

Scamp Another term for rough layout or mock ups.

Scoring The creasing of board to facilitate folding.

Scraper-Board A coated board with a specially prepared surface designed to produce crisp sharp lines amenable to printing in any process.

Screen The engraved glass or other material used to break up continuous-tone images into halftones for printing.

Sensitised A litho plate, when ready to print from, is 'sensitised'; it must be de-sensitised, otherwise the surface is subject to oxidization.

Sep An abbreviation on artwork – an instruction to blockmakers or platemakers to separate items into individual parts.

Separations Refers to various methods of separating colours on artwork.

Serif The finishing crossline point of a letter in type, usually classified as round, square, slab, etc.

Set The distance across the front of a piece of type.

Set-Flush Text matter set without indents.

Set-Off A term used to describe marks left accidentally on the opposite side of a piece of print, caused by wet ink.

Set-Solid Any matter set without leading between lines.

Shank Also called the body or stem, it is the side of the square of metal on which a typeface is mounted.

Side Head A heading positioned at the side of a page or column.

Silhouette The American term for cut out half tone.

Silk-Screen A method of printing produced by forcing ink through a silk or nylon mesh held in a frame. Parts of the screen are masked so that ink cannot pass through.

Slug A line of type cast in one piece.

Small Caps Capital letters, used to accentuate keywords.

Spine The bound edge of a book.

Split-Fountain Several colours printed in one impression and separated in the ink fountain.

Sorts Individual types, usually ordered in small quantities to print distinguished letterheads, etc.

Squared-Up Halftone A plate or block either rectangular or square.

S/S Abbreviated term for same-size. An instruction on artwork meaning actual size.

Stagger An irregular edge to a paragraph or typematter. Typewriter manuscript is staggered on the right as it is almost impossible to justify the right hand margin.

Stall-Date Advertising term meaning the date that an advertisement is due to appear.

Stat An abbreviation for photostat.

Static Natural electricity in paper.

Stereotype A duplicate block cast in metal from a matrix or flong. Only coarse work should be duplicated by this method, ie coarse screened halftones and plain type.

Stet Proof correction term for 'leave as printed'.

Stipple A technique in drawing where dots are applied by controlled spatter, or individually with a pen.

Glossary

Stem Another name for shank.

Tails The space at the bottom of a page where the page numbers or folios appear.

Text The greater part of type on a page and called copy in the advertising world.

Tissue Thin but fairly strong paper used for layout work.

Transparency A positive photographic image in colour.

Trim Cutting work to size, in printing, the trim size is given as a specification.

Type-Height The correct height of type measured from the feet (base) to the face. The standard is 0.9185.

Typography The setting of type in metal, photographically or in transfer form.

Tub-Sized A white cartridge paper suitable for drawing.

Umlaut Double dots over a character to indicate a vowel change in German

Uncial Large capitals handwritten, especially writings found in manuscripts of the fourth to the eighth centuries.

Unmounted Instructions to the blockmaker not to mount the plate on wood or metal.

Unopened edges Applies to books that have pages unopened by trim.

Upper Case Another term for capitals.

Velox American term for a screened photograph.

Verso The left hand pages of a book. Opposite to recto.

Vignette A photograph or half-tone with no definite edge. The background faded off to white.

Wash A continuous tone drawing usually produced with water-colour mediums.

Watermark A trademark produced in paper during manufacture.

Web-Offset The name of an offset press which prints from a reel or web of paper.

Glossary

Work and Tumble A piece of printed work repeated upsidedown on the reverse side.

Work and Turn A piece of printed work repeated the same way up on the reverse side.

Wrong Fount Type set in error which differs from the surrounding text.

X A marginal mark on a proof, meaning 'replace with a similar but undamaged character'. The letter to be altered should be encircled.

X-Height The height of the lower-case x in all type sizes.

Xerography A method of obtaining copies by electrostatic process.

Xography A trade name for simulated three-dimensional photographs.

Zinco A block etched on zinc

Index

Index